GLOBETROTTER™

Trave

G000081096

BULGARIA

KAPKA KASSABOVA

NEW
HOLLAND

NEW
HOLLAND

★★★ Highly recommended
★★ Recommended
★ See if you can

First edition published in 2008
by New Holland Publishers (UK) Ltd
London • Cape Town • Sydney • Auckland
10 9 8 7 6 5 4 3 2 1

website: www.newhollandpublishers.com

Garfield House,
86 Edgware Road,
London W2 2EA
United Kingdom

80 McKenzie Street
Cape Town 8001
South Africa

Unit 1, 66 Gibbes Street,
Chatswood,
NSW 2067
Australia

218 Lake Road
Northcote, Auckland
New Zealand

Distributed in the USA by The Globe Pequot Press,
Connecticut

ISBN 978 1 84537 564 5

Publishing Manager: Thea Grobbelaar
DTP Cartographic Manager: Genené Hart
Cartographer: Genené Hart
Editor: Nicky Steenkamp
Design and DTP: Nicole Bannister
Picture Researcher: Shavonne Govender

Reproduction by Resolution, Cape Town.
Printed and bound by Times Offset (M) Sdn. Bhd., Malaysia.

Photographic credits:
Tony Baker/International PhotoBank: page 36; **Pete Bennett**:
cover, pages 9, 12, 14, 21, 25, 28, 30, 40, 53, 63, 79, 83,
89, 91, 100; **Tom Cockrem**: page 49; **Philip Game**: page 26;
Anthony Georgieff: pages 11, 24, 44, 77, 81, 98, 114;
Kapka Kassabova: pages 15, 46, 62, 66, 67, 70, 71, 82, 84,
86, 101, 103, 104, 107, 112, 116; **Nigel McCarthy/Puffin
Images**: 4, 32, 34, 35, 39, 41, 61, 74, 85, 94; **Photo Access**:
pages 8, 13, 16; **Pictures Colour Library**: title page, pages 6,
7, 22, 27, 29, 37, 47, 48, 51, 56, 59, 65, 80, 97, 102,
108, 118; **Russell Young/Jonarnoldimages.com**: pages 18, 38.

Keep us Current:
Information in travel guides is apt to change, which is
why we regularly update our guides. We'd be grateful to
receive feedback if you've noted something we should
include in our updates. If you have new information,
please share it with us by writing to the Publishing
Manager, Globetrotter, at the office nearest to you
(addresses on this page). The most significant contribution
to each new edition will receive a free copy of the
updated guide.

Although every effort has been made to ensure that this
guide is up to date and current at time of going to print,
the Publisher accepts no responsibility or liability for any
loss, injury or inconvenience incurred by readers
or travellers using this guide.

Cover: The Cathedral of Assumption in Varna.
Title page: Women dressed in traditional Bulgarian folk
costumes.

CONTENTS

1
Introducing
Bulgaria

Bulgaria is one of Europe's few remaining secrets. One of the **oldest countries** on the continent, it sits on the **Black Sea** and on Europe's longest river, the **Danube**. The **Balkan Ranges** cross the country from west to east and give the peninsula its name. Layered with history and packed with stunning mountainous scenery, white sand beaches, medieval monasteries, and atmospheric old towns, it is still relatively unspoilt by mass tourism thanks to the obscurity that 45 years of totalitarianism ensured.

Bulgaria is the birthplace of the ancient civilization of the **Thracians**, and of legendary singer **Orpheus** and gladiator **Spartacus**. The world's first surviving **gold treasure**, 6000 years old, was found near Varna on the Black Sea. The **Cyrillic alphabet** was created in Bulgaria and adopted by other Slavic kingdoms. Despite its distinctive identity, Bulgaria is a **cultural hybrid**. Thracians, Romans, Bulgars, Slavs, Byzantines, Crusaders and Ottomans have sown their seed and built their empires here. And so Bulgaria's attractions combine exceptional natural beauty with the ruins of several major civilizations.

The laid-back capital **Sofia**, at the foot of Vitosha mountain, is a hotch-potch of architectural styles. The four majestic mountain ranges of **Rila**, **Pirin**, the **Rodopi** and the **Balkan Ranges** are dotted with towns of beautifully preserved architecture, **Eastern Orthodox monasteries**, and colourful **festivals**, Ancient fishing towns and modern resorts line the **Black Sea Coast**. The cities have the vibes of a European café society, while the dramatic countryside is seemingly frozen in time.

TOP ATTRACTIONS

*** Rila Monastery: the biggest monastery in the country.
*** Walking in Rila, Pirin, Rodopi Mountains or Balkan Ranges: spectacular scenery.
*** Bansko: historic mountain town with great skiing.
*** Tryavna, Koprivshtitsa, Etâra, Bojentsi: preserved period architectural villages.
*** Plovdiv Old Town: National Revival urban architecture.
*** Veliko Târnovo: seat of the Second Bulgarian Kingdom.
*** Sozopol and Nessebâr: ancient seaside towns.
*** The Black Sea: glorious white sand beaches.

Opposite: *Alexander Nevski Cathedral, Sofia.*

Above: *Rusenski Lom National Park is situated 20km (12 miles) south of the town of Ruse.*

Bulgaria is the European Union's newest member, a country in the throes of rapid transition, and Europe's new property hotspot. Her riches are bound to leave the first-time visitor surprised, intrigued, and somewhat wiser about what Europe means.

THE LAND

Bulgaria occupies the northeast part of the **Balkan Peninsula**, and its natural boundaries are the **Danube** to the north and the **Black Sea** to the east. Its neighbours are Romania, Serbia and Montenegro, the Republic of Macedonia, Greece and Turkey. A striking feature of its geography is the concentration of high mountains in the southwest: **Vitosha** just south of Sofia, **Rila**, the Alpine **Pirin**, and the older **Rodopi** ranges. Rila contains the **highest peak in the Balkans**, Musala at 2925m (9597ft), and Pirin the third highest, Vihren at 2914m (9561ft). The country's average altitude is 470m (1542ft) and mountain ranges take up about half of the territory, with 5% comprising high altitude ranges of above 1600m (5250ft). The country is dissected lengthwise by the enormous massif of **Stara Planina** (literally Old Mountain). It is also known as the **Balkan Ranges**, part of the Alpine-Himalayan chain, and measures 750km (466 miles) in length from its eastern end on the Black Sea coast to its western end on the Serbian border. To each side of the Balkan Ranges stretch massive plains: the fertile **Danubian plain** to the north (its eastern part, Dobrudja, is locally

STATISTICS

Official name: Republic of Bulgaria
Area: 110,993km² (68,968 sq miles)
Population: 7.7 million
Population growth rate: 0.86 (2006)
Capital: Sofia, population 1.5 million (2007)
Second city: Plovdiv, population 377,000
Highest mountain: Rila, at 2925m (9596ft)
Longest river: Danube
Official language: Bulgarian
Official religion: Eastern Orthodox Christianity
Currency: the Lev (BGL)

known as 'the granary of Bulgaria') and the **Thracian plain** to the south. Sandwiched between the Balkan Ranges and the low, long ranges of **Sredna Gora** is the **Rose Valley**, known for its rose cultivation and its patented rose oil.

Although the Danube is the only navigable river, hundreds of **rivers** spring from the mountains, crisscross the country and flow into the Black and Aegean seas. They also offer opportunities for rafting, canoeing and fishing. Bulgaria is dotted with over 300 natural lakes, of which the largest are those near the Black Sea coast, and the most spectacular are the crystalline **glacial lakes** in Rila and Pirin, such as the **Seven Rila Lakes**. Mineral and water springs abound, and so do spa resorts and mineral baths: **Sandanski**, **Hissarya** and **Stara Zagora**. The **Black Sea** is a closed, non-tidal sea and its 378km (235-mile) Bulgarian coastline has two large bays which contain the coast's major towns, **Burgas** and **Varna**. The seacoast has expansive white sand beaches and well-developed tourist amenities – from purpose-built holiday resorts to atmospheric, ancient towns like **Sozopol**, **Nessebâr**, **Varna** and **Balchik**.

Climate

Bulgaria has a moderate continental climate, which means that seasons are well defined. Most times of the year are fine for visitors, depending on what you plan to see and do. Winters (November to February) are cold, dry and snowy; temperatures may fall below 0°C, especially in the mountains where -20°C (-4°F) is not uncommon. Spring is unstable, as in the rest of Europe, and often brings rain and changeable temperatures. Summer is hot but not excessively so: temperatures in high summer (July–August) are usually around the 28–30°C

Below: *Bulgaria is the ideal place for a skiing holiday in winter.*

(82–86°F) mark, but higher in the north. In higher altitudes, especially in the Alpine landscape of Pirin, the sun and heat can be harsh. The autumn months of October and November are generally rainy but mild, and particularly beautiful in the parks, forests and mountains as deciduous trees turn gold and red. Stara Planina divides the country into the semi-Mediterranean south and the continental north, and in the winter its canyons serve as channels for the harsh northern winds.

Plant Life and Wildlife

Bulgaria has some of the richest plant life in Europe. It is home to several **nature reserves** and **national parks** with over 3550 higher plant species, including 68 species of **orchids** alone, and protected mammals such as the **brown bear**, the **wolf**, the **golden jackal**, the **wild cat**, the **Golden and Imperial eagles**, and 37 species of reptiles. The largest reserves are the **Balkan National Park**, which contains several self-regulated eco-systems, and the UNESCO-protected **Pirin National Park**. The UNESCO-protected **Srebârna Biospheric Reserve** near Silistra in the north boasts 150 species of marsh birds. **Eco-tourism** and **conservation** gathered pace in the late 1990s, and there are now excellent organized eco-tours (walking, hiking or cycling) run from big cities like Sofia and Varna. They focus on specific reserves and regions with rare wildlife and plants. For more details, see the sections on Rila, Pirin, the Rodopi and Central Bulgaria.

HISTORY IN BRIEF

Bulgaria has undergone a long and turbulent history thanks to its location at the always busy crossroads of Europe and Asia. Great Barbarian hordes and great empires have clashed, built and destroyed here. Periods of stagnation – the centuries-long Ottoman rule, the totalitarian decades – have alternated with times of national revival and cultural effervescence. Bulgaria's fate through the centuries has in turn been colourful, glorious, tragic and, in its later stages, heavily marked by the interests of Europe's Great Powers.

The Thracians

Drawings, tools and necropoli from early Bronze and Iron Age inhabitants have been found in the Magura cave in the northwest, near Stara Zagora, Varna and many other places. Some of the prehistoric peoples were probably Thracians. In any case, the first ethnically distinct tribe who pitched up camp in the region and stayed for the long haul were the **Thracians**, well established by the middle of 2000BC. To this day, the southern region of Bulgaria is called Thrace. The populous Thracians formed a hardy civilization, but since they didn't leave many written records, all references to them come from ancient Greek and Roman sources: Herodotus, for instance, believed them to be the most numerous people in the (known)

ORPHEUS

Orpheus is the most famous Thracian. His birthplace is believed to be in the Rodopi. Orpheus's singing was legendary, but it is the tragic story of his love for Eurydice that has inspired composers and writers. Distraught at his wife's death, Orpheus went looking for her where no living mortal goes – the Underworld. His desperate plea touched even the heartless god Charon, and Orpheus's wish was granted – provided he didn't turn to look back as Eurydice followed him back to earth. But of course he looked, and Eurydice's ghost vanished forever. Soon after, the poet met his grisly end. While playing his lyre, a party of entranced Bacchanalians descended on him and tore him to pieces.

Left: *A monument dedicated to the founders of Bulgaria.*

HISTORICAL CALENDAR

6000BC Neolithic and Palaeolithic tribes inhabit the region.

2000BC Thracian tribes well settled in today's Bulgaria.

5th–3rd century BC Odrysian Kingdom of Thracians, first capital Edirne, Turkey, second capital Seuthopolis, Bulgaria.

AD46 The Roman Empire occupies Thrace.

Late 5th century The nomadic Bulgars arrive.

Early 6th century The Slavs arrive.

681 Han Asparuh unites Bulgars and Slavs in the First Bulgarian Kingdom.

863 Tsar Boris I adopts Christianity as national religion.

893 The Slavonic script based on the alphabet of brothers Cyril and Methodius is adopted.

893–967 Bulgaria under Tsar Simeon I reaches territorial hegemony in Southern Europe and a 'Golden Age' of culture. Capital moves from Pliska to Preslav to Ohrid (Macedonia).

1018–1185 Byzantine occupation.

1185–1246 The revolt of the brothers Petâr and Asen leads to independence. Second Bulgarian Kingdom with capital Târnovo becomes a major European power.

1393 Christendom in southeast Europe is too disunited to resist the invading Turks. Bulgaria falls to the Ottoman Empire and her longest dark hour follows.

1762 Beginning of the National Revival period.

April 1876 The unsuccessful April Uprising against the Ottomans ends with the slaughter of civilians.

1877–78 Russian-Turkish war.

3 March 1878 Liberation of Bulgaria from Ottoman rule and San Stefano Treaty.

July 1878 The Treaty of Berlin revokes the San Stefano Treaty and partitions Bulgaria. Alexander of Battenberg becomes independent northern Bulgaria's first Prince.

6 September 1885 The Treaty of Berlin is annulled unilaterally by Bulgarian politicians, and the country is unified.

1886 Ferdinand I of Saxe-Coburg-Gotha replaces Alexander of Battenberg as Prince.

22 September 1908 Tsar Ferdinand declares complete independence from Turkey.

1912 First Balkan War. Bulgaria, Greece and Serbia fight the Turks for the liberation of Macedonia.

1913 Second Balkan War. Bulgaria fights Greece, Serbia and Romania for Macedonian territory and suffers massive defeat.

1915 Bulgaria joins the Central Powers in a bid to regain lost Macedonia – and suffers enormous losses again.

1918 Tsar Ferdinand abdicates in the face of popular discontent and his son Tsar Boris III takes over. Bulgarians have to live with Macedonian terrorists, Communist terrorists, and the security forces of the right-wing government.

1941 Faced with the advancing German army, a militarily weakened Bulgaria joins the Axis. Despite Nazi pressure, Bulgaria refuses to declare war on Russia or deport its Jewish population.

1943 Tsar Boris dies suddenly after a visit to Hitler and his six-year-old son Simeon is crowned.

9 September 1944 The Soviet Army invades Eastern Europe. Bulgaria capitulates. The Communist-led Fatherland Front usurps power. Mock trials and executions of 'enemies of the people' follow.

1946 The People's Republic of Bulgaria is established, after a rigged referendum which annuls the monarchy. The surviving Royal family is exiled to Egypt, then Spain.

1954 Todor Jivkov becomes first secretary of the Central Committee of the Bulgarian Communist Party.

1962 Todor Jivkov is elected Prime Minister.

1984–89 Anti-Turkish government campaign of forced name-changes and displacement. Hundreds of thousands of Bulgarian Turks emigrate to Turkey.

10 November 1989 Todor Jivkov is overthrown in a bloodless coup inside the government.

1990 Andrei Lukanov, a 'reformed' Communist (assassinated in 1996), becomes PM. Several changes of government follow, and a painful shift to market economy.

1997 Mass protests against the Socialist government which resigns. The Union of Democratic Forces is elected.

2004 Bulgaria joins NATO.

January 2007 Bulgaria joins the European Union.

world. For thousands of years, the Thracians did brisk trade with neighbours in Asia Minor and the Aegean. Their culture had strong Hellenistic elements, and their elaborate gold and silver treasures speak of a sophisticated civilization. The height of Thracian civilization was the Odrysian Kingdom in the 5th–3rd centuries BC, with its second capital in Seuthopolis, near Kazanlâk. In 350BC, Thrace was overrun by the Macedonians of Philip and Alexander, territorial boundaries shifted, and shorter-lived Thracian kingdoms sprung up and died.

Roman Times

Inevitably, the Romans made their presence known, and eventually took over Thrace in the mid 1st century AD. Once the Romans were running Thrace, they laid down excellent roads (Via Militaris, the biggest military road in the Balkans, passed through Plovdiv/Trimontium), administered some splendidly well-appointed towns like Trimontium and Augusta Trayana/Stara Zagora, and Thrace prospered for three hundred years. Traces of this fruitful time can be seen today in Sofia, Plovdiv, Hissar, Sozopol and Stara Zagora. But as the vast Roman Empire split into its Western and Eastern parts, it also became more vulnerable than ever to incursions from **Barbarian tribes** to the north and east. From the 3rd century AD, great wild hordes descended from Asia Minor and the Russian steppes onto the Balkan Peninsula. The face of Roman Thrace soon changed, as different Barbarian tribes pillaged the towns and dispersed the Romanized Thracians. By the time those other Barbarians, the **Slavs** and the **Bulgars**, turned up, the Thracian civilization was all but extinguished – though the Thracian people blended in with the newcomers.

Bulgars and Slavs

The ethnic origins of the nomadic people who gave Bulgaria its name are debated by scholars. It is most

Below: *The Thracian King Seuth III.*

Below: *Icon painting in Bulgaria started officially with the adoption of Christianity in 863.*

likely that the Bulgars were an ethnic amalgam of Altaic and Turkic tribes from Central Asia. Their migration to the Caspian and Black Sea regions of Europe began in the 2nd century and continued for four hundred years, often in military alliance with the Huns. In 480, Byzantium formed an alliance with the Bulgars and successfully crushed the Goths, but the Bulgars showed no intention of becoming Byzantine allies thereafter. In the 5th and 6th centuries, they frequently made incursions into an already weakened Byzantine Thrace. In the centuries-long confusion and violence of the great migrations, the Bulgars' equestrian skill gave them a military edge. The Bulgars were first unified into a very large state by Khan Kubrat in 632, in what is today the Ukraine. After Kubrat's death, his son **Khan Asparukh** decided to move his people to the more fertile, warmer lands south of the Danube, where the Slavs had been living for about a century. The Slavs and the Bulgars had a common enemy – Byzantium – and while the Slavs were numerous, the Bulgars had horse power. The foundations of the **First Bulgarian Kingdom** were thus laid, and in **681** Byzantium recognized Khan Asparukh's independence. Bulgaria became the first state in Central and Eastern Europe.

First Bulgarian Kingdom

The new kingdom led to a defensive policy against Byzantium and an expansive policy in all other directions. Under Khan Krum (802–814) and later Khan Omurtag, the Bulgarian kingdom established its capital in **Pliska** (northeast Bulgaria), occupied all of modern Romania and Macedonia, and had its sights firmly set on the greatest regional prize – Constantinople. **Christianity** became an official

religion in 863 under the Byzantine patriarchy, and the power of the visionary statesman Tsar Boris I was consolidated.

A turning point was when the Thessaloniki-born brothers Cyril and Methodius created a new alphabet for the Moravians and the Bulgarians, to counter Latin and Greek cultural domination. The monks' Bulgarian students, Konstantin in Pliska and Kliment in Ohrid (today Macedonia), set up influential literary schools and adapted the Glagolithic script into the **Cyrillic alphabet** (893), which consolidated the culture and literacy of the Slavonic world forever.

Above: *A mural depicting Russians routing Bulgarians in a cavalry skirmish.*

Under the Constantinople-educated **Tsar Simeon** (893–967) Bulgaria led a long, mutually devastating campaign against Byzantium, which established Bulgaria as a European superpower and stretched its territory to include the Peloponnesus and Serbia. This was also the '**golden age**', a period of great cultural and economic efflorescence, and Bulgaria's finest hour. Darker times followed as Byzantium invaded in 1018 and stayed for over a century.

Second Bulgarian Kingdom

Eventually, a revolt led by the *boyar* (feudal lord) brothers Petâr and Asen in 1185 resulted in an independent **Second Bulgarian Kingdom**, with Petâr II as its Tsar and **Târnovo**, their family fortress, the new capital. After the assassination by infighting *boyars* of both Asen and Petâr, their brother, Tsar Kaloyan (1197–1207) of Wallachia and Bulgaria, took the reins and smartly obtained protection

THE BULGAR MIGRATIONS

The original nomadic Bulgars from Central Asia ended up all over Europe. Although some of them eventually formed a kingdom in the Balkans and gave their name to modern Bulgaria, others stayed in Armenia, Ukraine and Russia, or migrated further west to Lombardia and were absorbed into what became northern Italy. Today, Italian names like Bulgarini and Bulgari retain echoes of the great migrations.

Above: *A sign in Cyrillic script.* **Opposite:** *Rila Monastery murals.*

from Pope Innocent III against the invading Hungarians. But the Pope was no help against Kaloyan's new neighbours: the knights of the Fourth Crusade. They spelt the end of old Byzantium and a new chapter in Bulgaria's defence and expansion. The politically astute Tsar Ivan Asen II came to the throne in 1230, and through a mix of negotiations with the Latins, political marriages, and campaigns against the incoming Tatars, he created a regional superpower which occupied three quarters of the Balkans. Trade and culture flourished in the wisely run kingdom.

The Ottomans

But in the 14th century, internecine intrigues and feudalization weakened Bulgaria and its Balkan neighbours. The disunited forces of European Christendom proved no match for the new superpower invading from the East: the Ottoman Turks. The battle of Kosovo Polje, where Sultan Murat defeated the Serb army, and the battle of Nikopol on the Danube, where the Ottomans routed the ill-prepared Crusaders, set the tone for Bulgaria's next five centuries. The capital, Târnovo, fell in 1393 after a three-month siege. The Bulgarian state and nation were destroyed. The Ottoman occupation lasted five centuries and retarded the civilizational development of Bulgaria as a European country. Only glimpses of the Renaissance and the Enlightenment penetrated through the 'iron curtain' of medieval Islamic colonialism. Though the Ottomans' achievements on their own turf were magnificent, their civilizational energies did not spread far into their Balkan provinces; but dogma and taxes did. However, those who converted to Islam were spared taxes, and aside from periods of violent Islamizing campaigns, the Turks were tolerant occupiers. Though culturally Bulgaria was for centuries a stagnant Ottoman backwater, economically it thrived thanks to trade within the Empire. This prosperity culminated in the National Revival.

CYRILLIC

In January 2007, Cyrillic became the European Union's third official alphabet, alongside Latin and Greek. Cyrillic was the indirect creation of the Byzantine-born brother monks Cyril and Methodius who invented the Glagolithic script in the 850s. There is some controversy about the final version of Cyrillic. It was either the work of Clement of Ohrid, a Bulgarian student of the brothers, or of the Preslav Literary School during medieval Bulgaria's Golden Age in the early 10th century. Either way, the adoption of Cyrillic changed the face of the Slavonic world, and Cyril and Methodius became patron saints of Slavonic literacy and culture. Today, the alphabet is used by Slavic countries like Macedonia, Serbia and Montenegro, Russia, Ukraine, Belarus, and by several Central Asian countries including Kazakhstan and Mongolia.

National Revival and Independence

In the second half of the 18th century, as the Ottoman Empire declined, Bulgaria began to emerge unto its own Rennaissance. The National Revival was sparked by the work of educators like the monk Paisii Hilendarski who in 1762 wrote the first national 'Slav-Bulgarian History' and travelled across the country to teach the people who they were. **Monasteries** like **Rila** and **Bachkovo** became repositories of Revival literature, religious art, icon-painting schools, and revolutionary meetings. As commerce with Western Europe and the Ottoman Empire peaked, a powerful class of wealthy, nationally minded merchants appeared. They had their children educated in Western Europe, and built handsome houses, schools, and public buildings in what is now called National Revival style – you can see examples in most towns and villages, especially in Plovdiv, Koprivshtitsa, Tryavna, Arbanasi and Bansko. Education and self-knowledge went hand in hand with a hunger for freedom, and the leaders of the independence struggle soon emerged from the gifted young elite: Vassil Levski, Georgi Rakovski, Todor Kableshkov and the poet Hristo Botev. The first attempt at independence, the **April Uprising of 1976**, erupted prematurely in Koprivshtitsa and ended in horror. Most of the leaders and 30,000 civilians were massacred by the Ottomans. The slaughter shocked Europe and gave Russia and Austro-Hungary an excuse to attack 'the sick man of Europe', as the Ottoman Empire was known, and extend their own zones of influence. The **Russo-Turkish War of 1877–78** ushered in Bulgaria's independence.

The Wars

Things didn't go too well after the forced partitioning of the new state (*see* panel,

BLOOD TAX

The most painful form of taxation the Ottomans inflicted on their Balkan provinces was the 'blood tax'. This meant taking young boys from Christian families, converting them to Islam, and training them as top warriors in the elite corps, the Janissary units. The Janissaries were unleashed on the same civilian populations from which they were taken, and were notorious for their cruelty and fanaticism. But by the 17th century, the Janissaries had become too powerful, a state within a state, impossible to control by the Sultan. They ended up undermining the Empire by extorting money, abusing power, refusing to modernize, and even assassinating sultans who challenged them. In 1826, Sultan Mahmud II decided enough was enough, and forcibly disbanded the Janissary units by dispossessing, executing and exiling them.

on page 18). The first King, 22-year-old German prince and former officer in the Russian army Alexander of Battenberg, was soon overthrown for the more capable Prince **Ferdinand I of Saxe-Coburg-Gotha** in 1886. The ambitious Ferdinand was obsessed with regaining Macedonia and restoring Bulgaria to its San Stefano size. He dragged the country into a disastrous 1913 war with its neighbours (the Second Balkan War), followed by World War I in which he joined the Central Powers. Both resulted in catastrophic human and territorial losses for Bulgaria, especially after the punitive 1919 **Treaty of Neuilly** clipped Bulgaria of large chunks of land and handed them to Greece and Yugoslavia. Macedonia was once again completely lost. Broken, Ferdinand abdicated in 1918 in favour of his son Boris. But the capable **Tsar Boris III** inherited a political mess he did his insufficient best to control. The interwar years were turbulent as the vexed 'Macedonian question' and the rise of militant

LEVSKI

Many streets, stadiums and even a top soccer team are named after the revered Vassil Levski (1937–73), a.k.a the Apostle of Freedom, Bulgaria's most remarkable independence leader. He was a progressive, selfless visionary who believed in the values of democracy, education and self-reliance. A lapsed monk, a self-taught intellectual and a trained legionnaire, Levski lived much of his short and ascetic life in hiding, and many inns, monasteries and houses served as his shelter. A monument in Levski Square, near Alexander Nevsky Cathedral in Sofia, marks the spot where he was hanged by the Ottoman authorities only five years before independence, after being denounced by a fellow Bulgarian. His comrade-in-arms, poet Hristo Botev, wrote a hauntingly bleak requiem to enslaved Bulgaria to mark his execution, soon after which he himself perished in battle with the Turks.

Right: *Bulgarians of the 19th century.*

Communism undermined an otherwise thriving, striving state. Bulgarians had to live simultaneously with Macedonian terrorists, Communist terrorists, and the brutal security forces of the right-wing tsarist government.

Then **World War II** erupted, and the Bulgarian government opted for siding with the advancing Germans, to avoid devastation. One good thing came out of this alliance: the salvation of the Bulgarian Jews and the relatively small loss of civilian life. Sofia and other towns in Central Bulgaria were, however, heavily bombed by the Allies, and thousands perished in air-raids. Macedonia, already part of Yugoslavia, was occupied by Bulgarian forces, but ultimately not regained – another reason for joining the Axis. Tsar Boris's sudden death in 1943, believed to be caused by poisoning at Hitler's hands, left a vacuum as his six-year-old son Simeon was crowned.

When in **September 1944** the Soviet tanks rolled in, the anti-Fascist resistance movement, united in the Communist-led party Fatherland Front, took control with Stalin's blessings. Two years and many thousands of executions of 'enemies of the people' by 'courts of the people' later, a rigged referendum removed the monarchy. The Royal family fled, the secret police executed large numbers of the intelligentsia, and tortured and killed 'public enemies'. The malformed **People's Republic of Bulgaria** was born.

Communism

Prime Minister of the sinister new Republic became **Georgi Dimitrov**, a Moscow-trained Comintern (international Communist movement) ideologue. He was hero of the famous 1933 Leipzig Trial staged by the Nazis and won for the Comintern by Dimitrov's impassioned self-defence – his last worthy act. Dimitrov's face appeared on bank notes, and when he died in 1949, his mummified body appeared in Sofia's Mausoleum, Lenin-style, to be visited by generations of puzzled school children.

The people of the People's Republic suffered greatly for the next 45 years. Labour camps inspired by the Soviet gulags were set up to receive any opposition – real or imag-

THE 'BULGARIAN UMBRELLA'

The notorious 1978 case of 'the Bulgarian umbrella' in London was one of many political murders and kidnappings said to have been committed by the Bulgarian State Security with KGB help. The victim was the 37-year-old dissident writer and broadcaster Georgi Markov who had defected to London in 1969. He was stabbed near Waterloo Bridge with an umbrella containing a ricin pellet, and died soon after. The prime suspect is a Danish/Italian mercenary, alive and well somewhere in Europe, but the mastermind was allegedly the KGB. Nobody has been prosecuted over Markov's death. In 1991 a Bulgarian general destroyed the 17-volume secret files on Markov. He served a sentence for this later. At his trial, he explained that the files had 'contained nothing important'.

Above: *The Parliament building in Sofia.*

ined – to the Soviet-styled government. Secret agents spied on everyone, private property was 'nationalized', i.e. confiscated, and the thriving agrarian economy was industrialized in brisk, brutal 'five-year plans'. The Soviet puppet government of Chervenkov adopted an isolationist policy, followed by the 35-year-long dictatorship of the mediocre but cunning Party apparatchik **Todor Jivkov**. Shortages became part of life, though it was never a question of dire deprivation – the 'Mother Party' provided the bare essentials.

Bulgaria was the USSR's most loyal satellite and one of the Eastern Bloc's drabbest regimes – though not its cruellest. Unsurprisingly, in the 1950s there was a mass exodus of ethnic Jews, Armenians and Turks. The ethnic Bulgarians of course weren't allowed to go anywhere, and defectors' families were severely punished with dispossession, exile and loss of civil rights.

Bloodless Revolution and Democracy

Gorbachov's *glasnost* and *perestroika* took the ossified Jivkov government by surprise and steeled its resolve to cling to power. The regime looked for ways to distract the citizens from the winds of change blowing over Eastern Europe. The 1980s saw the catastrophic **anti-Turkish campaign** of name-change, which resulted in Bulgaria's entire ethnic Turkish minority – a million souls – being displaced, brutalized, and mass-emigrating to Turkey in the largest European migration since World War II. The massive loss of labour force further paralysed an already stagnant economy. The fledgling opposition party, **Eco-glasnost**, could not be crushed by the regime, and in November 1989, Bulgarians woke to a peaceful **coup**. Jivkov was ousted by his own comrades, and the exhilarating, traumatic 1990s began.

Unlike some of its neighbours, Bulgaria remained a peaceful civil society throughout the 1990s, though the

Yugoslav war crippled it economically. The transition to a **market economy** has been very painful for the older generation and for those who lost their jobs in Socialist-run factories, without compensation or employment prospects. A huge brain-drain of the highly skilled to Western countries started in the 1990s and has only recently slowed down, with some expats and graduates returning to the bigger towns.

The New Bulgaria

In January 2007, after centuries of feeling painfully isolated from the continent, Bulgaria joined the **European Union**. This historic move is not without its critics, both at home and elsewhere in Europe, as its consequences are yet to be understood by Bulgarians and other Europeans wary of more Eastern European migrants. But there is no doubt that EU membership will only speed up the progress made in the difficult 17 years since the fall of the regime, and will give Bulgarians the confidence and the optimism that a century of political upheaval and economic hardship had robbed them of. Despite ongoing social and economic problems, today Bulgaria is one of Eastern Europe's most stable and vibrant societies.

GOVERNMENT AND ECONOMY

Since 1990, Bulgaria has been a **parliamentary republic** with a President and a Prime Minister who heads the Council of Ministers for a four-year term. The Prime Minister is elected by the **National Assembly**, itself elected by proportional representation every four years. It is not surprising that no government has been re-elected since 1989: the reforms that each government has had to implement – or failed to implement – have been so painful that most voters have felt bitterly disillusioned.

Political life post-1989 has swung between the **Bulgarian Socialist Party (BSP),** which was simply the revamped Bulgarian Communist Party, and the

Below: *The flag of Bulgaria is a tricolour consisting of three equal-sized horizontal bands of white, green and red.*

A PLACE IN THE SUN

Bulgaria is the fastest growing property market in Europe. Most foreign buyers focus on the seaside and ski resorts like Bansko, but many are also buying in the Veliko Târnovo area as well as in small villages with little infrastructure, where old houses go – or rather went – for a song. If you are thinking of buying, choose a real estate agency jointly run by Bulgarian and British experts; there are several of these in Sofia, Veliko Târnovo and elsewhere. The explosion of the real estate market and the impressive upgrade of the seaside and ski resorts have helped open Bulgaria economically and socially. But some developers' greed and some foreigners' lack of care are endangering nature and creating deforestation and erosion problems, especially along the overdeveloped seacoast.

YES OR NO

A Bulgarian shaking or wobbling her head agrees with you. Nodding her head downwards while saying 'ts' means no. This cultural peculiarity is an endless source of bewilderment for foreigners. To further confuse things, some Bulgarians will use the Western system of head shaking and nodding, to help you. Of course this doesn't help you at all because you don't know when it's done. One way to avoid constant confusion is to learn that 'da' means yes, and 'ne' means no, and not to rely too much on body language.

right-wing **Union of Democratic Forces (UDF)**, an intellectuals' opposition party against the regime. The unpopular Socialists were toppled by the UDF in 1991, but the UDF's lack of political expertise became painfully obvious when it foundered only a year later and was replaced by a caretaker government, giving way once again to the Socialists in 1994. The early and mid-1990s were raw years of political instability and everyday deprivation: power and water cuts, extremely high unemployment, mass emigration, bankruptcies, and hyperinflation which in 1996 reached 580%. This hardship sparked off mass protests in 1997 which threatened to destabilize the country. The Socialist government resigned and was replaced by the UDF government of the capable Ivan Kostov, ushering in a relatively stable period of fixed currency board and economic growth.

The big political surprise came in the form of Bulgaria's **exiled King Simeon Saxe-Coburg-Gotha**, who made a triumphant return in 2001 and was greeted by desperate crowds who elected his eccentric party, National Movement Simeon II, with him as Prime Minister. Simeon betrayed the nation's expectations with his unfulfilled promises and paternalistic attitude, but his party's four-year 'reign' improved Bulgaria's international image and oversaw its NATO membership and EU road map.

After Kostov's government failed to be re-elected, the UDF fragmented into a myriad small parties, creating a space for the new beast on the block – the ultranationalist, neo-fascist Ataka. In late 2006, the former Socialist leader Georgi Parvanov became the first President to be re-elected since 1989, but close behind him came the leader of Ataka. Ataka's credo is in direct conflict with modern European values in general, and with the **Movement for Rights and Freedoms** in particular – a popular party representing ethnic minorities.

Bulgaria isn't rich in natural resources. In 1997 more than a third of Bulgarians were living in poverty, now down to 13%. The **urban economy** of technology and retail is booming and unemployment in Sofia is low at around 9%, but many small towns are depressed and depopulated, with dismal infrastructure. Until 1990, massive quantities of fresh produce were exported throughout the Eastern bloc, and agriculture continues to play a role in the economy, though the focus today is on exporting **wine**. Bulgaria has gradually moved away from environmentally suspect industries to **technology** and **tourism**. In addition to **electricity**, of which it is the biggest exporter in the region, **tourism** and **property investment** from abroad have become its fastest growing industry.

Above: *The Palace of Justice in Ruse.*

THE PEOPLE

Modern Bulgarians are the result of inter-racial mingling among the three main ethnic groups that have lived here: **Thracians**, **Slavs** and **Bulgars**. Unlike predominantly Slavic nations, they are closer in appearance to South Europeans: typically of medium build, with dark hair and olive skin. Ethnic Bulgarians make 84% of the population, followed by 9.4% of ethnic Turks, 4.6% of Roma, and smaller numbers of Armenians, Jews and Greeks.

Bulgarians have always aspired to Europe. The Bulgarian sense of national identity is a mixture of vague pride in the glorious ancient and medieval civilizations of these lands, and on the other hand a sense of insecurity brought on by the decades of poverty and social and cultural isolation. Frustration and anxiety at having been repeatedly partitioned by the Great Powers and kept away from Europe by two anti-European, retrograde empires – the Ottomans and the Soviets – still haunts the collective memory. This is why Bulgaria's EU accession has been an important symbolic gesture of acceptance into the club for this capable nation.

NAMES

Names matter in Bulgaria. Almost everybody has a name-day, celebrated as a mini-birthday on the day of the corresponding saint – Gergyovden or St George's Day for example is the name-day of everyone named Georgi. Those with names related to flowers celebrate on Palm Sunday, here known as 'Tsvetnitsa' or Flowers' Day. People have three names: their given name, their family name, and their middle name or patronymic, after their father's first name. Women's surnames always take an extra 'a', which is the female marker at the end of nouns as well.

Society

Once dubbed by an exasperated Russian prince 'the Prussians of the Balkans', the Bulgarians are indeed stubborn and hard-working, but they are also self-critical, sceptical and fatalistic, not given to extreme passions. There have been no full-blown civil conflicts here since the Middle Ages. Bulgaria is one of the least nationalistic and most tolerant societies in Eastern Europe and has treated Armenians, Jews, and – except for the state terror of the 1980s – ethnic Turks as equal citizens. But an ugly new trend has appeared, reflecting an overall European tolerance for far-right factions: a patriotic, aggressive Eastern Orthodox fundamentalism bordering on ultranationalism. The accompanying racism doesn't directly affect visitors of other races, as the energy of neo-fascist party Ataka is focused on the indigenous Turks and Roma, and on denying the Holocaust – thus attempting to bring anti-Semitism into Bulgarian society for the first time in history.

Most people live in their own apartments and houses. The nuclear family is still strong, although people typically can't afford more than one child. A new fad for full-time mothers and a second child has emerged among moneyed couples, but most couples stop at one child rather than compromise on a decent lifestyle. This, combined with brisk emigration in the 1990s, has resulted in one of the world's lowest birth rates.

Women enjoy successful careers, entirely to their own credit in a macho society. Communism gave women 'equality', but it also required them to work full-time while also running the household as traditional housewives. Fortunately, Bulgarian women, more so than their men, are resourceful and versatile. This doesn't apply to the decorative girlfriends of the

Below: *A shepherd near the town of Kazanlâk.*

mutri – broad-spectrum gangsters who wielded too much power in the 1990s but are now on the wane.

Around 80% of Bulgarians live in urban areas, and the contrast between the countryside and big cities like Sofia and Varna is startling. Infrastructure and wealth are concentrated in the cities where big companies are based. A new middle class is emerging, very slowly bridging the gap between the new rich and the numerous dispossessed underclass. Those who live well are the highly educated, sometimes foreign-educated, professionals employed by companies; small business owners; and people in the hospitality industry. Those who live really well tend to be 'businessmen' (which could mean anything from a high-powered gangster to the legitimate owner of a software company), some politicians (who are sometimes also 'businessmen'), and entertainers. Those at the bottom are the sick, the unemployed, people made redundant in the early 1990s and now unemployable, professionals on horrifyingly low state salaries, and pensioners surviving on 60 euro a month.

Language

Bulgarian was the first Slavic language to be written in the Cyrillic alphabet. As a South Slavic language, it is mutually understandable with Serbian. The good news is Cyrillic shares some letters with the Latin alphabet; the bad news is only a few letters like 'a', 'e', 'o' and 'k' are actually identical, while the rest can be misleading. Сувенири for example doesn't quite look like 'souvenirs', or България like Bulgaria. Most words in Bulgarian are Slavonic, but a few thousand everyday words come from the Bulgars and the Turks. Some 20th-century words are borrowed from German, French and English. Although Bulgarian is spoken by everybody, Turkish is a first language for the ethnic Turks, and other languages are used by the smaller minorities: Romani, Armenian, Hebrew. There are also Armenian and Turkish-language schools and newspapers. Bulgarians are linguistically able, and the 20th-century tradition of having language schools (the American College in Sofia is 145 years old) has paid off: the well-educated under-40s

THE BULGARIAN MUSLIMS

There are two groups of Muslims in Bulgaria. The Pomaks are Slav Muslims, a remnant from Ottoman times when some Christians chose Islam over slaughter or heavy taxes. They are considered a religious but not an ethnic minority, and many of them live in the Rodopi region – you'll spot their bright headscarves and baggy trousers. The Turkish Muslims, also a remnant from Ottoman times, make for 9.4% of the entire population and are concentrated in the south and around the Shumen area in the northeast. In the 1980s there was a senseless terror campaign against them by the regime, cynically dubbed 'the Revival process', which shattered many lives. Today, the Bulgarian Turks are represented by the Movement for Rights and Freedoms led by politician Ahmed Dogan. There are Turkish-language broadcasts on TV and Turkish-language newspapers and schools.

BULGARIA'S JEWS

The fate of Bulgaria's 50,000 Jews during World War II deserves to be better known. In the monstrous chronicles of the Holocaust, it is the only story of an entire Jewish community with a happy ending. But only just. The Bulgarian war-government, headed by King Boris II, was undecided on Jewish matters and concerned with placating its Nazi masters. It was the population, headed by dignitaries and influential individuals, who vocally opposed the deportation of a single Jew. The Jews were seen simply as fellow Bulgarians. The Bishop of Plovdiv promised that if the trains left, he would lie on the tracks. That constant Nazi pressure and rampant European anti-Semitism did not disfigure Bulgarian society is a remarkable achievement. The 14,000 Jews in Bulgarian-occupied Macedonia, however, paid the deadly price of deportation.

speak at least one foreign language. Don't expect, however, to be greeted in flawless English when you buy a tram ticket at a kiosk or take a taxi.

Religion and Customs

Eastern Orthodox Christianity, the official religion of Bulgaria, has prospered since the fall of Communism. Under the Ottomans, Eastern Orthodox Christianity meant national identity, and helped the Bulgarian people survive as an ethnos. Under Communism, religion was all but banned, and practising Christians were intimidated – though the regime couldn't bring itself to close down all the churches, since they were part of the cultural heritage. A wave of religious fervour swept across the country post-1990: once again Bulgarians have turned to religion for extra strength in uncertain times.

Eastern Orthodoxy is highly dogmatic and resistant to reform, and its practices are unique in several ways. The chant-like services can seemingly last for hours while the congregation, bowing, cross themselves from right to left with the three first fingers gathered. Singing replaces the Western organ here, and the Slavonic liturgies sung by male choirs during festivals like Easter are heavenly.

Right: *An abbot at the Kalofer Monastery. It has been in operation since 1640.*

Candles are bought at the entrance, then lit inside: those for the dead are placed in low sand pits, while those for the living go above. The result is smoke-damaged frescoes (as in the Russian Church in Sofia). The special place of **icons** in spiritual culture shows how Christianity and pagan superstition blend in many Bulgarian customs: people visit monasteries for the miraculous powers of the resident icon, which they kiss and give offerings. The customs of the painted Easter eggs – the first painted one must be red, for health – and midnight Mass to announce the resurrection of Christ are a similar blend.

The many colourful festivals reflect the seasonal nature of a rural lifestyle now all but lost. Fortunately, the food and the celebrations remain. A pagan custom surviving from Thracian times are the splendid *kukeri* processions in late winter and early spring in Shiroka Lâka, Koprivshtitsa, Blagoevgrad and smaller towns. These scary mummers in animal masks and cattle bells act as exorcists of evil spirits and harbingers of fertility. Another Thracian ritual is the mystical *nestinarstvo* or fire-dancing, originating in Strandja in the southeast, and now commercialized. On **Gergyovden**, St George's Day, the patron saint of livestock, whole lambs are spit-roasted. The Dyonisian-inspired festival **Trifon Zarezan** celebrates wine-making with – predictably – feasts and large quantities of wine. On **Christmas Eve** an odd number of vegan dishes must be placed on the table, and food is left overnight for the spirits of the dead. Bulgarian folklore abounds in all manner of supernatural beings, mostly from Slavic superstitions: *samodivi* (nymphs-cum-witches), *zmeyove* (dragons), *karakondjuli* and *talasumi* (vampires). Look out for these in church frescoes.

Culture and Art

Bulgaria has a rich **ethnographic heritage** which creatively blends elements from Thracians, Slavs, Bulgars and the Orient. The mind-boggling range of regional costumes and customs can only truly be appreciated in small mountain towns like Bansko where traditional dress is still worn by old women, or in ethnographic museums like the marvel-

Above: *Painted Easter eggs, Etâra.*

ICONS

The icon is central to Bulgarian artistic culture. In the Middle Ages, iconography was the only fine art form, and modern secular portraiture at the end of the 19th century was the natural extension of the icon. Churches are heavily adorned with icons, with the patron saint's icon occupying a place of honour. Some icons have incalculable value: the 10th-century *Three-handed Virgin* at Troyan Monastery, the early 14th-century *Silver Virgin* at Bachkovo Monastery. Some of the best places to see valuable collections are the Alexander Nevski Crypt in Sofia, the Tryavna Museum of Icons and the Bansko Permanent Icon Exhibition. Icons by modern artists are usually copies of existing ones and range from the crude to the exquisite, reflected in the price.

Opposite: *Bulgarian cuisine.* **Below:** *Embroidery, Arbanasi.*

lous Smolyan Museum. The **artisan** traditions and products you'll come across are centuries old and reflect the old ways of life and the Bulgarian peasant aesthetic: densely woven woollen accessories, aprons, socks and felt rugs; embroidery and fine lace; heavy medieval-style silver and copper jewellery with filigree motifs; glazed ceramics and pottery in earthy colours, still widely used in cooking; leather and fur hats, bags, belts and saddles; copper vessels; musical instruments. You can watch artisans at work in Etâra, Tryavna, Veliko Târnovo and Dobrich Ethnographic Complex. **Icon-painting** is very much alive, and so is **modern art**, showcased in the many commercial and museum art galleries of Sofia, Plovdiv, Veliko Târnovo and all other bigger towns.

Music is where Bulgarians have reached greatest artistic heights. Bulgarian **folk music**, which gained popularity in the 1980s with a series of international recordings, is renowned for its vocal pyrotechnics, special techniques of vocal vibration and harmonies, and hair-raising complex melodies. The human voice is worshipped above all, but the epic, piercingly sad sound of the **100 *kaba gaidi*** or 100 bagpipes is also unforgettable when heard in the open air. Folk music continues to evolve thanks to big international and national festivals and modern treatments by classical, jazz and pop musicians. The BBC world music award-winning **Ivo Papasov** and the vocalist **Yildiz Ibrahimova** perform an eclectic mix of Bulgarian, Gypsy, Jewish and Turkish music, while musicians like *kaval* (Balkan flute)-player **Teodossi Spassov**, percussionist **Stoyan Yankulov** and vocalist **Elitsa Todorova** blend jazz, ethno and rare folk instruments into new

musical forms. In keeping with its musical tradition, Bulgaria has been producing world-renowned classical musicians: opera singers **Boris Hristov**, **Raina Kabaivanska**, **Gena Dimitrova** and **Ana Tomova-Sintova**; violinists **Mincho Minchev** and **Vasko Vassilev**, jazz musician **Milcho Leviev**. Today, the nation's favourite music is the *chalga* – a blend of sublimely vulgar Orientalized turbo-folk with crude lyrics, performed by scantily clad divas. Chief among them is an exotic, cross-dressing Roma, Azis, a.k.a 'the King of *chalga*'.

Food and Drink

Bulgarian cuisine combines Balkan, Middle Eastern and Central European foods to very tasty effects. It uses fresh local produce, so it's always best to eat what's in season. Bulgarians are big on salads, and within 10 minutes of arriving, you'll run into the ubiquitous **shopska salata**, a tomato, cucumber and onion salad topped with *sirene* (Bulgarian white cheese from cow's or sheep's milk). **Roast peppers** and **aubergines** are a staple and turn up as salads, *kyopolu* or *lyutenitsa* (spread or side dish). Tasty, no-nonsense vegetarian dishes include **lentil soup** and **bean stew**, and stuffed vegetables which come in meat and veg varieties: *sarmi* (stuffed vine or cabbage leaves), stuffed peppers, tomatoes and aubergines.

But this is a land of carnivores. Lamb, pork and chicken are the favourites, and there are two main ways of cooking meat: roasting or grilling, and slow-cooked casseroles. The first method produces the ever-popular *kyufteta* and *kebapcheta* (grilled meatballs with spices and herbs) and *shish* (skewered meat). These are served at stands, fast-food joints and simple *mehani* (tavernas), with salad and French fries. Far more exciting are the casseroles,

Above: *A Bulgarian casserole.* **Opposite:** *Bulgaria's leading core pilsner is slightly bitter and tart.*

LACTOBACILLUS BULGARICUS

In 1905, in a Geneva laboratory, the Bulgarian biologist Stamen Grigorov identified the bacillus that made fresh milk ferment into yoghurt. Scientists named it *lactobacillus bulgaricus* after him. Around the same time, the Nobel prize winning Russian scientist Mechnikov researched the effects of yoghurt on health and longevity, and discovered that Bulgarians had the highest life expectancy among 36 countries. He puts this down to their lively consumption of yoghurt. Yoghurt continues to be a staple of the Bulgarian diet, but mysteriously, the life expectancy of Bulgarians has dropped.

---

traditionally slow-cooked in earthenware dishes called **gyuvech**: it could be anything from a seasonal vegetable stew to a meat and vegetable stew, or even a block of herbed, baked *sirene*. There are regional varieties of the **kavarma**, a type of casserole with meat, vegetables and red wine, topped with an egg. The indulgent **Bansko kapama** (see panel, page 49) is the queen of casseroles. As in Greece and Turkey, **mussaka** is a staple. Animal innards are honoured too, including fried livers and **shkembe chorba**, a vinegar-garnished tripe soup reputed to be a cure for hangovers. In Bulgaria **seafood** is usually served plain, and although on the seacoast you'll have reasonable fish (ask that it's fresh and not frozen), don't expect it to be anything more exciting than grilled or fried with potatoes on the side.

Locally made **natural yoghurt** is some of the best in the world, although at some restaurants you might well face its inferior cousins (containing starch). If it's not dense and fatty, it's no good. In southern Bulgaria, you can get buffalo and ewe yogurt sold in jars by local producers. Bread (**pitka**)– either with yeast or soda – is traditionally white and delicious, but sadly, many restaurants serve boring sliced bread. You might be asked how many slices (**filiiki**) you want; request them toasted just in case. **Banitsa**, layered filled pastry, is traditionally made with cheese and eggs, but also comes with spinach, leeks and sweet fillings like pumpkin or apple. It is always delectable home-made, but rather greasy in the shops, as are most dough- or pastry-based snacks except the **gevrek** (savoury bagel). The local flat salami **lukanka** comes in many regional guises; it is flavoursome and meat-packed, and usually eaten as an entrée or drink accompaniment.

Cafés and pastry shops offer a good choice of Western-style cakes and ice creams, but traditional desserts are thin on the ground and almost all Ottoman-influenced. Some sweet treats to look for: **yoghurt with honey or fig jam**, **apple strudel**, **pumpkin strudel**, **baklava**, *ashuré* (sweetened boiled wheat with nuts). One of the few places in the country with a range of such delights is the Oriental Patisserie in Plovdiv. The local mountain teas and the traditional Turkish coffee (easier to find in the south) are delicious, but displaced in the big towns by the ubiquitous espresso. The **mineral water** is predictably fabulous in a country full of natural springs.

Locally made **alcohol** is excellent and extremely good value. **Wine-making** has a long tradition here (the Thracians were great imbibers), and although the Communist regime did its best to destroy the industry, it's now back on track and producing some top-notch wines in five distinct vine-growing regions. Among the best **beers** are Kamenitsa, Zagorka, Shumenska and Astika. Whisky and vodka are popular, but the local spirit is the industrial-strength plum or grape brandy **rakia**, drunk straight and always consumed with a salad, pickles, or *lukanka* and cheese. Many restaurants and cafés offer freshly squeezed juices.

2
Sofia

Nestled against the dramatic backdrop of **Vitosha Mountain** at an altitude of 545m (1788ft), Sofia enjoys the paradox of being one of Europe's youngest independent state capitals and **one of the oldest European capital cities**. Its changing fortunes are reflected in the hotch-potch of urban styles. While Sofia's human history goes back to the 7th century BC, modern Sofia was born at the end of the 19th century as capital of free Bulgaria. This explains the *fin-de-siècle* design of many buildings and the Viennese yellow tiles paving the official centre. The unmistakable creations of Communism stand out, but they are mercifully sparse in the city centre, allowing the inner city to retain an old-worldly charm and laid-back atmosphere. A dozen **old churches**, **a mosque** and **the Balkans' largest Sephardic synagogue** overlook this 21st-century cityscape of peeling *belle époque* façades and swanky new hotels and banks. And underneath it all, in the underpasses, lie the remains of the Roman city of Serdica.

Sofia is a pleasant city to loiter in, and its lively centre can be seen on foot in half a day. Stay longer to include a day trip to Vitosha, see museums and galleries, chill out in parks and dine in style. Most attractions, hotels and shopping are east of the main commercial artery, **Vitosha Street**, which is closed to traffic except for trams. It runs south to the South Park and north to the Railway and Bus stations, and borders the distinctly Communist-era **National Palace of Culture**, the Balkans' biggest convention centre. The listed order of attractions can be used as a sightseeing guide.

DON'T MISS

*** Alexander Nevski Cathedral: an architectural and artistic masterpiece.
*** A chair-lift or **gondola ride** to Vitosha.
*** Visit one of the top museums: the Archaeological Museum, the National History Museum, the Ethnographic Museum and National Art Gallery, or the National Gallery for Foreign Art.
** Loiter: people-watch from street cafés and sit in city parks.
** Dragalevtsi Monastery and Boyana Church: priceless pieces of medieval Bulgaria hidden in the forest.

Opposite: *Sofia's tramway system was built in 1901.*

Alexander Nevski Cathedral ★★★

The most monumental historical building of Sofia, and the largest Orthodox church in the Balkans, Alexander Nevski was built almost entirely with enthusiastic citizens' donations to commemorate the fallen Russians in the Russo-Turkish war which liberated Bulgaria from the Ottomans in 1877–78. The five-nave basilica was named after Prince Nevski of Novgorod, whose relics (a piece of bone) are kept in a gold box in the church. The church's architectural style majestically combines the Northern Russian Orthodox tradition, which you can spot in the splendid golden domes, and neo-Byzantine elements. It boasts 12 bells, the heaviest of which weighs 12 tons, and when they toll, you can hear them from Vitosha Mountain. The church was built with materials from three continents and artwork by five painters. In addition to Bible scenes and the icon of St Alexander Nevski, note the two icons near the entrance depicting Tsar Boris I and St Cyril and St Methodius. The two thrones before the altar were for the royal family (hence the crown) and for the Patriarch. At the inauguration of the Cathedral, Tsar Boris III was absent due to a terrorist alert. Fifty metres (164ft) high and with a capacity of 5000, the cathedral's acoustics are particularly suited for large choirs and concerts. Bulgaria's renowned opera singer Boris Christov made recordings here. **The Crypt** houses extraordinary icons from around the country, from the 12th century onwards (see panel, page 33). Ask the in-house museum guide about the historical background. Open 07:00–19:00 every day.

Below: *The Alexander Nevski Cathedral is a cross-domed basilica featuring an emphasized central dome.*

National Gallery for Foreign Art ★★★

This sumptuous, 18-hall collection housed in a Baroque building features priceless art from around the world. From Japanese prints, African masks,

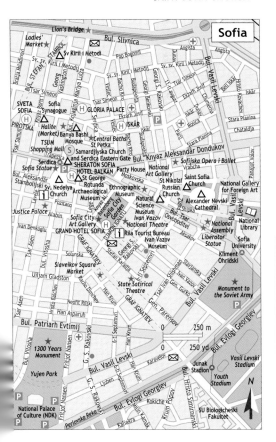

Indian miniatures and Buddhist art to Picasso, Rodin and early European masters, this is a must for art lovers. The gallery also hosts contemporary art exhibitions. Open 11:00–18:00, closed Tuesday.

St Sofia Church ★★

One of the oldest buildings in Sofia, and the source of the capital's modern name, the three-nave basilica St Sofia survives from the time of the Byzantine Emperor Justinian in the 6th century. Its changing faces trace the changing fortunes of Serdica-Sofia – a hiding place from Barbarian

DECODING THE ICONS

Alexander Nevski's crypt icons have meanings hidden to the naked eye. Note the double image of Archangel Michael and Archangel Gabriel announcing the immaculate conception. Gabriel is considered the female side of our nature, while Michael is the male. Together, they form a whole. Such doubling-up of saints is unique to Bulgarian iconography. Moreover, Christ (known as Pantocrator in the Eastern Orthodox canon) is always depicted as a detached, upright figure, immune to suffering. Only his eyes are 'allowed' to express emotion and human-like states, like the 13th-century Christ Pantocrator (left as you enter). Two icons of St George have a small figure behind the saint wearing the janissary uniform: a Bulgarian boy marked as a janissary but saved by St George. Here, the Bible meets medieval history.

Right: *The St Nikolai Russian Church was built in 1914.*

What's in a Name

Sofia's motto is 'She grows but never ages' – a fair call for a city of many lives and names. In 7th century BC the Thracian tribe Serdi gave it its first recorded name, **Serdica**. Under the Romans in the 1st century AD it became the thriving **Ulpia Serdica**, until its devastation by the Huns in the 5th century. Rebuilt under Byzantine Emperor Justinian and renamed **Triaditsa**, it was part of both Bulgarian Kingdoms and given the Slavic name **Sredets**. The name **Sofia**, meaning wisdom in Greek, originated in the 14th century from the eponymous church, the oldest in the city and probably inspired by the Agia Sofia in Constantinople.

incursions into the city, a metropolitan church, a necropolis, a mosque with minarets, a superstitious no-go area after an earthquake, a gas storehouse – until it was finally restored in the 1930s. To the right of the altar you'll see a memorial to Christians persecuted by the Communist state. Outside is the fire of the Unknown Soldier, the grave-boulder of iconic 19th-century writer Ivan Vazov, and a memorial to the saviours of Bulgaria's Jews, a copy of which exists in Jerusalem. Open every day 07:00–19:00 in summer, 07:00–18:00 in winter.

National Assembly ★

This small but perfectly formed neo-Renaissance building has witnessed many state-run processions in the Communist years and protests in the 1990s. The words above the entrance say 'Unity is strength'. The equestrian statue in the square depicts **the Liberator** Alexander II, the Russian Tsar who declared war on Turkey and brought Bulgaria independence.

St Nikolai Russian Church ★★

Built in 1914 by a Russian architect, this fairy-tale church in the Northern **Russian Orthodox** style stands out with its green-tiled, gold-capped domes. It replaced an existing mosque and is dedicated to St Nikolai the 'miracle maker'. Its interior is sadly blackened by candle smoke, but its gilded altar gate remains a highlight. It sits in the City Park, a good place to relax on a bench. Open 08:00–18:30, Sunday 08:00–17:30.

National Art Gallery Museum and Ethnographic Museum ★★★

Beautifully placed in the former **Tsar's Residence**, this fine collection traces the evolution of **Bulgarian art** from iconography to secular art through its various 20th-century movements. Remarkable masterpieces by major artists are on display: look out for Vladimir Dimitrov Maistora, Zlatyu Boyadjiev, Tsanko Lavrenov and Dechko Uzunov for an insight into past and present Bulgaria. Open 10:00–17:30, closed Monday.

The eastern wing contains the **Ethnographic Museum**, a rich collection of ethnic artefacts and costumes, and a good introduction to the Bulgarian way of life through the centuries. There is a good souvenir shop and captions in English. Open 10:00–17:30, closed Monday.

SOFIA SYMBOL

Across from the Sheraton Hotel and the Presidency stands Sofia's heaviest woman and latest symbol: a 4-ton, 24m (79ft) tall statue of Saint Sofia. The anatomically correct and not very saintly gold-fleshed woman in black robes holds the wreath of fame and the owl of wisdom, and is crowned as the Greek goddess of fortune Tyche. Pertinent symbols – in Sofia's past life this spot was 'graced' by a statue of Lenin and, many centuries ago, by a statue of Apollo.

Left: The National Art Gallery, in Sofia, has one of the country's richest early Revival period collections.

SOFIA MARKETS

Sofia is dotted with food markets, but most of them are in neighbourhoods. There are two main inner-city food markets: **Halite** and **Ladies' Market**. Halite is an attractive indoor market in the Central European style, and Ladies' Market just behind it is an unstructured event where peasants come to sell their produce by the kilo. **Slaveikov Square** has a bustling open-air book market, and you can buy fresh fruit and homemade yoghurt further down the tramline along **Graf Ignatiev**. There is an antiques and curios market in **Alexander Nevski Square**. Subway passages are cheap commercial hubs, good for souvenirs.

Sofia City Art Gallery ★★

Next door to the National Theatre, this former casino houses excellent permanent and visiting exhibitions from Bulgarian and foreign modern artists. Free entry.

Archaeological Museum ★★★

Housed in Sofia's first mosque, the 15th-century Buyuk (Big) Mosque, this enchanting collection follows the Bulgarian lands' historic progression – from mammoth remains to Hellenic statues, Thracian treasures like the curious Valchitran gold from the 14th century BC, Roman sarcophagi, the perfectly preserved floor mosaic of St Sofia Church, the column recording a 30-year peace treaty between Bulgaria and Byzantium, memorial columns from Khan Omurtag (*see* panel, page 40), and the original famous icon of St Teodor Stratilat from the medieval capital Veliki Preslav. English-language guides are available. There's a pleasant café in the garden. Open 10:00–18:00 every day in summer, 10:00–17:00 and closed Monday in winter.

St George Rotunda ★★

The ancient-looking building in the courtyard of the Presidency building really is ancient. Dating from the

Right: *The St George Rotunda is considered to be the oldest preserved Roman building in Sofia, dating back to the 4th century.*

2nd–4th centuries, it is the **oldest preserved Roman building** in Sofia. The inside is remarkable for its thick layers of stripped and painted-over murals, reflecting the changing times. Under Sultan Selim in the 1500s it was converted to the **Giol Mosque**, and Christian murals were painted over with Islamic plant motifs, a tiny fragment of which still survives the subsequent stripping off after Independence. Some fresco fragments from the 6th and 10th centuries were revealed in the process (the big-eyed angel at the base of the dome is 11 centuries old). Try to catch the evening vespers at 17:00, when seminarists pray in the characteristic chanting style of Bulgarian Orthodoxy. Open 08:00–18:00 every day.

Above: *The Banya Bashi Mosque is one of the oldest mosques in Europe.*

St Petka Samardjiyska Church and Serdica Eastern Gate ★

In the underpass across from the Sheraton and the Presidency stands a small stone building. St Petka Samardjiyska Church, built in the 14th–15th centuries, has no towers, windows or bell tower and is underground because the Ottomans didn't allow Christians to decorate their religious buildings or build them higher than a metre above ground. The church's valuable 15th-century frescoes are still visible. In the subway, you will also find the eastern gate of the Thracian-Roman city Serdica.

Banya Bashi Mosque and Central Baths ★

Strategically located next to the Central Baths, Banya Bashi, 'the Baths Mosque', is the only functioning

mosque in Sofia. Built in 1576 by the architect of Istanbul's Blue Mosque, it is stylized in the then typical Islamic style, and remarkable for being Bulgaria's only domed building on a square base. Next door are the early 1900s neo-Byzantine **Central Baths**, set to reopen as Sofia's City Museum and a spa centre in 2007. Mosque open 09:30–22:30 every day.

Above: *The Sveta Nedelya Church is an Eastern Orthodox church in Sofia.*
Opposite: *Just half an hour's drive from Sofia, Vitosha National Park is home to a multitude of species.*

Sofia Synagogue ★★

The beautiful six-vaulted Sofia Synagogue sits 'conveniently' across from the mosque. Designed by an Austrian architect in 1905–09, it is the **largest Sephardic Synagogue in the Balkans** at 33m (108ft) high and seating 1200 souls. Its classical Judaic features are fused with Moorish and Byzantine decorative elements. The massive Viennese brass chandelier weighs 1700kg (3749lb). It was in a shabby state until interior restoration began in 2002. The **Museum** outlines the history of Bulgaria's Jews (*see panel, page 24*). Open Mon–Fri 09:00–16:00, lunch break 12:30–13:30; always ring the doorbell.

Sveta Nedelya Church ★★★

The epitome of harmonious Eastern Orthodox architecture, St Nedelya stands plump with its five naves at the very centre of Sofia and Roman Serdica. Damaged in 1853 by the Turks, it was restored with citizens' donations in an Orthodox Renaissance style, until a terrorist attack shook its foundations and killed 200 people in 1925. The bomb was planted by a Communist group and aimed at Tsar Boris III. He was lucky not to be there, but his ministers' families were killed. The church has valuable icons and a rich interior. Open 07:00–18:30 every day.

SOFIA SPRINGS

One of the reasons Sofia has been inhabited for so long is the thermal and cold mineral springs in the area. Sofia residents believe in mineral water's medicinal properties. In central Sofia, the place to fill your bottle is at the Central Baths. If you want to soak, Pancharevo Lake in Vitosha has a mineral pool and baths complex.

AROUND SOFIA
Vitosha National Park ★★★

Vitosha, the mountain just south of Sofia, covers 300km² (190 sq miles) of land rich in wildlife and rivers. It is a popular weekend and ski destination, and a good escape from traffic pollution. Easily reached from the city by taxi or bus, it is ideal for walking, berry-picking, skiing, or a panoramic chair lift or gondola (cabin lift) ride. The gondola leaves from the village of **Simeonovo**, and the chair lift from **Dragalevtsi** village. **Aleko** is one of two main tourist bases from where you can reach the brooding **Cherni Vrâh** (Black Peak), 2290m (9514ft) high and excellent for the steep trek or ski-ride down. Vitosha's symbol is the *moreni*, enormous boulders which flow down the slopes like stone rivers. **Zlatni Mostove** (Golden Bridges), the other main base, has the most spectacular *moreni*. It can be reached after several hours' trekking from **Boyana** village, by bus from town, or a 2–3-hour trek from Aleko. There are also three worthwhile sights at the doorstep of Vitosha: Boyana Church, the National History Museum and Dragalevtsi Monastery.

ROMAN SOFIA

Emperor Constantine the Great referred to Ulpia Serdica as 'my Rome'. His Rome lies right underneath central Sofia. The underpass of the Sheraton Hotel and the Presidency contains Serdica's eastern gate, while the indoor food market Halite (across from Banya Bashi Mosque) is built on top of a marketplace thousands of years old. The Halite subway contains Roman baths and remnants of the city wall. An amphitheatre, a Zeus temple and more gates have been found nearby, and excavations continue around Sofia.

Above: *The Boyana Church consists of three buildings. The first church was built on the eastern side in the 10th century.*

Boyana Church ★★

Set among old pines and open after decades of restoration, this is one of Europe's oldest churches and a UNESCO heritage sight. Built in the 11th–12th centuries during the Second Bulgarian Kingdom and restored three times before 1900, it is tiny but contains exquisite frescoes. The pictorial style heralds the early **Italian Renaissance**. The two most famous frescoes are the striking portraits of the church patrons, **Sevastokrator Kaloyan** and **Dessislava**, and opposite them, the Bulgarian Tsar and Kaloyan's cousin, Constantin Assen and his wife. Part of the church was used as a sepulchre for Kaloyan's family. Restoration work continues. Guided tours in English or German. Open daily 09:30–18:00, 09:00–17:30 in winter.

National History Museum ★★★

Set in a panoramic spot opening up on Vitosha, the former residence of dictator Todor Jivkov offers a comprehensive journey through Bulgaria's rich history and is well worth a few hours. Here you can see (if they're not on tour) the

---

KHAN OMURTAG

In the National History Museum's lobby, you will find a wall inscription which copies the original inscription left in the early 9th century by young Bulgaria's progressive ruler Khan Omurtag. 'Well though we may live, we die and another is born. May the one born tomorrow remember the deeds of the one before.' The original, longer inscription was found on a stone column in the Forty Martyrs' Church in Veliko Târnovo as late as the mid-19th century.

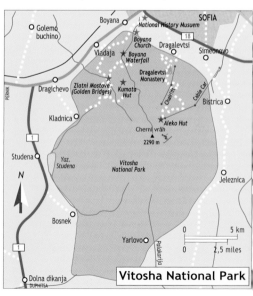

Vitosha National Park

famed 4th–3rd-century BC **gold treasure of Panagyurishte**, the 4th-century BC **silver Rogozen treasure**, and others from the Bronze Age. The spacious hall dedicated to medieval history gives you a glimpse into medieval art, Cyrillic literature, and the rise and fall of the two Bulgarian Kingdoms. The shop offers an excellent selection of guidebooks and souvenirs, and the outside café offers little choice but priceless views. Open daily 09:30–18:00.

Dragalevtsi Monastery ★★

This distinctive red-striped monastery was built in 1345 under Tsar Ivan Alexander, only decades before the Ottomans arrived. After the Turkish invasion, its monks were forced out, but in the 15th century a local *boyar* (feudal lord), Radoslav Mavar, restored it. He and his family are depicted inside the Monastery Church of the Virgin Mary of Vitosha, and all the other frescoes are also survivors from that time. The paintings are a 17th-century addition, and the church was further expanded in 1932. The monastery operates as a convent, and the church is staffed by nuns. The stone house outside the complex is the Patriarch's occasional residence. Open daily 08:00–18:00, lunch break 12:00–13:30 (ring bell if closed).

THE HAPPY MAN

Aleko, the popular tourist base on Mount Vitosha, is named after the progressive satirist Aleko Konstantinov, a.k.a Shtastlivetsa, the Happy Man. He initiated the first public ascent of Mount Vitosha in 1895, when 300 men and women from Sofia trekked up to Cherni Vrâh. This marked the beginning of Bulgaria's tourist movement. Aleko Konstantinov is the author of the classic *Bay Ganyu*, a devastating satire of the Bulgarian peasant upstart, and a pioneering travelogue about America, *To Chicago and Back*. He was assassinated at age 34 for criticizing the Tsarist government.

Below: *The Dragalevtsi Monastery is situated at the foot of Vitosha Mountain.*

Sofia at a Glance

Best Times to Visit

Sheltered by the Vitosha ranges, Sofia's air is still, which worsens the smog. Winter (Nov–Mar) can be bleak and soggy, and advanced summer (July–August) stiflingly hot and dusty, with temperatures rising above 30°C (86°F) and the locals fleeing to the countryside. Spring is lovely, and autumn is beautiful, mild, and less wet. Late spring/early summer and early autumn are the best times to enjoy Sofia, while Vitosha is best in the snowy winter, colour-struck autumn, and summer when the butterflies and berries come out.

Getting There

Many European airlines fly to Sofia, including Bulgaria Air which also connects Sofia with Varna and Burgas. Charter flights are cheaper, and Bulgarian Air Charter flies from Northern Ireland, France, Germany, Israel and Eastern Europe. The train from Istanbul or Athens/Thessaloniki is a comfortable option, as are the buses. The E79 road from Greece through Kulata is in excellent condition. The picturesque E87 from Turkey to the Black Sea coast passes through Strandja Mountain. The E80 from Turkey to Sofia is scenic and runs through Plovdiv. From the Black Sea, the most interesting way to get to Sofia is by bus.

Getting Around

The easiest way to get around Sofia is by taxi. Look out for the cheaper 1280 taxis, otherwise check the tariff on the side window before you get in; it shouldn't be more than 50 stotinki per km. Sofia's public transport is reliable and cheap. To find out where buses and trams run, get the red Sofia City Map from a kiosk or the stalls in Slaveikov Square. Bus 93 leaves from Hladilnika terminus for Dragalevtsi, and buses 63 and 64 go to Boyana. Vitosha Street is serviced by trams, convenient for getting to the Central Railway and Bus Stations. Buy tickets from kiosks or drivers for exact amounts, and punch them inside.

Where to Stay

The hotels suggested here are in the city centre. Sofia is much dearer than the rest of the country, but the mid-range is still good value by European standards. Cheap hotels cluster around Lions' Bridge.

Luxury

Grand Hotel Sofia, 1 Gurko St, tel: (02) 811-0800, fax: (02) 811-0801, reservations@grandhotelsofia.bg www.grandhotelsofia.bg New luxury hotel with huge rooms, ideally located next to Sofia City Garden.

Sheraton Sofia Hotel Balkan, 5 Sv Nedelya Sq, tel: (02) 981-6541, fax: (02) 980-6464, sofia.Sheraton@luxury collection.com www.luxury collection.com/sofia Smack in the centre of things opposite St Nedelya Church, luxury at its most decadent.
Gloria Palace, 20 Mariya Luiza Blvd, tel: (02) 980-7895, fax: (02) 980-7894, Gloria_sof@spnet.net www.gloriapalacehotel.bg Central, close to Halite, good value.

Mid-range/Budget

Sveta Sofia Hotel-Restaurant, 18 Pirotska St, tel: (02) 981-2634, svetasofia@abv.bg www.svetasofia-alexanders.com Set in pedestrian shopping street. Disability-friendly. 'VIP' apartment has panoramic views.
Niky, 16 Neofit Rilski St, tel: (02) 952-3058, niky-92@internet-bg.net www.hotels-bg.com/niky Off Vitosha St, convenient, business-oriented, summer garden.
Baldjieva, 23 Tsar Asen St, tel/fax: (02) 981-2914. Small, comfortable hotel in quiet spot west of Vitosha St. Breakfast included.
Hotel Iskâr, 11b Iskâr St, tel: (02) 986-6750, hoteliskar@dir.bg www.hoteliskar.com Homely rooms and apartments with wooden furniture in central neighbourhood near Halite.

Sofia at a Glance

WHERE TO EAT

Sofia has become a hip place to eat and drink, with a huge range of folk-themed restaurants, simple eateries, pizzerias, bistros, European restaurants, world food restaurants, all excellent value.

Opera, 113 Rakovski St, tel: (02) 988-2141. Under the Opera House. Trendy, elegant restaurant-bar. Fine European food, great desserts and wines. Sofia's yuppies love it.

Uno Enoteca, 45 Vassil Levski Blvd, tel: (02) 981-4372. Fine Mediterranean cuisine and wines in rock garden, very popular.

Before and After, 12 Hristo Belchev St, tel: (02) 981-68. Good bistro food in exquisite former house of poet Mara Belcheva. Tango on Sundays.

The Veggie Home, 10 Patriarch Evtimii St, tel: (02) 981-5677. Superb dishes and fresh juices in central but quiet setting.

Checkpoint Charlie, 12 Ivan Vazov St, tel: (02) 988-0370. Hip restaurant with an East-West Berlin theme, good bistro food, live jazz.

Manastirksa Magernitsa, 67 Han Asparuh St, tel: (02) 980-3883. The 'Monastery Kitchen' serves traditional recipes in charming garden and cosy indoors.

Pri Yafata, 28 Solunska, tel: (02) 980-1727. Bulgarian dishes with folk décor and live music.

Vodenitsata, Dragalevtsi, next to chair lift, tel: (02) 967-1058. Touristy folk-themed restaurant, '**The Mill**', offers excellent national dishes and live music.

SHOPPING

Vitosha St is for the international brand shopper. The Mall TSUM across from the Sheraton offers up-market Bulgarian and European retail. Visit the Refan shop here for natural soaps with rose petals. Halite across the road has quality and health foods. Pirotska St next door is a pedestrian mall ending with the Ladies' Market. For books in Bulgarian, English and German, go to Book Centre in 52 Pirotska St or the Slaveikov Sq stalls. From there, Graf Ignatiev St along the tramline offers miscellaneous shops, including Orange for books and music. Solunska St has some good fashion retail stores. Shishman St, between Graf Ignatiev and the National Assembly, is lined with funky boutiques and gift shops. For crafts and souvenirs, the Ethnographic Museum has a good shop, or try Traditional Crafts Souvenir Shop at 4 Parij St (before Alexander Nevski Cathedral). Alexander Nevski Square is the place to browse for antiques, curios and icons. Chushkarcheto Carpet House at 38 and 193 Rakovski St has hand-woven carpets. While you're in Rakovski St, check out the art galleries.

TOURS AND EXCURSIONS

You do not need a tour guide to see Sofia and Vitosha. Nearby attractions like Rila Monastery are within easy reach by bus or car. For tours further afield, there are some tour operators who cater for small groups and individuals. The following three share the address 20B Stambolijski Blvd (entry from Lavele St):

Bulgarian Association for Alternative Tourism (BAAT), tel: (02) 980-7685, baat@spnet.net and **Zig-Zag Holidays**, tel: (02)980-5102, www.zigzagbg.com offer tailored and specialized tours. **Odysseia-in** (www.odysseia-in.com) offer rural holidays, bird-watching, monastery visits and all manner of adventure and cultural travel. **Spatia Tours** (at 2 Slaveikov Sq, tel/fax: (02) 986-1212, http://wildlife.spatial-tour.com) specialize in wildlife and mountain tourism.

USEFUL CONTACTS

Central Bus Station, tel: 0900 21000 (24 hours), check www.centralnaav togara.bg for timetables.

Avis Car Rental, tel: (02) 988-8167, Sheraton Hotel.

Tany 97 Car Rental, tel: (02) 963-3083, www.tany97.com

Rila Bureau for purchasing train tickets, 5 Gurko St.

Police, tel: 166.

3
Rila and Pirin

Rila and Pirin in the southwest are Bulgaria's highest and most dramatic mountains, rich in wildlife and history, and containing between the two of them a staggering 350 lakes. In the winter they become busy **ski hubs**, and the rest of the year they are heaven for **hikers** and **nature-lovers**.

Rila has the Balkans' **highest peak, Musala** (2925m/9596ft), and exceptional natural beauty which culminates in the **Seven Rila Lakes**. The spectacular **Rila Monastery** is Bulgaria's largest monastery and a centre of national consciousness and religious art.

Pirin National Park peaks at Vihren (2914m/9560ft), the third-highest point in the Balkans. At the southwest of these Alpine peaks you'll find the 'sand pyramids' in the wine-growing **Melnik** region. Seen from another enclosure of medieval Bulgarian culture, the nearby **Rojen Monastery**, they form a dramatic, desert-like foreground to the snow-capped Pirin ranges behind, and one of the most interesting scenic contrasts in the country.

The distinctive towns of **Melnik** near the Greek border and **Bansko**, the skiing and hiking gateway to Pirin, have an idiosyncratic local culture. This region is historically known as **Pirin Macedonia** and had the misfortune of being the last Bulgarian chunk of the Ottoman Empire to gain independence, and therefore becoming involved in the bloody Balkan wars. The towns' fortified period architecture, cobbled streets, old churches, wealthy merchants' houses and cosy taverns offer an accessible glimpse into the variety of Bulgarian regional cultures.

DON'T MISS

★★★ Rila Monastery: Bulgaria's largest monastery and a symbol of spiritual resilience.
★★★ Hiking in **Rila Mountain** and the **Seven Rila Lakes**.
★★★ Skiing or hiking in **Pirin National Park** near Bansko.
★★★ Bansko's old town: fortified Revival houses and traditional women's clothes.
★★★ Melnik: wine tasting and sand pyramids.
★★ Rojen Monastery near Melnik: unusual frescoes and panoramic lookout point.

Opposite: *Colourful murals of Rila Monastery.*

Above: *Monks' cells double up as tourist accommodation.*

Rila Monastery ★★★

Shrouded by mountain mist at 1150m (3772ft) in Rila Mountain, Bulgaria's largest and most decorated monastery demands at least a few hours to be appreciated.

It was founded in the 10th century by the hermit Ivan Rilski and over the centuries became an influential cultural centre in the Second Bulgarian Kingdom. All that is left of its medieval glory is the **Hrelyuva Kula**, the fortified tower in the courtyard, built in 1335. In the 15th century, the monastery was sacked and closed by the Ottomans, but only decades later, it was rebuilt by the local community. In the first half of the 19th century, the monastery complex was expanded and painted by some of Bulgaria's best icon-painters and wood-carvers, from the Bansko and Samokov schools. In 1833, disaster struck again in the form of a fire which nearly destroyed the monastery. It was quickly rebuilt with generous donations from locals. In the northern wing, the blackened original kitchen, *magernitsa*, used to cater for monks and pilgrims. Judging from the size of the cauldrons, there must have been many hungry mouths. You could easily spend half a day in the glorious courtyard exploring the scenic monastery surrounds and lunching in one of the simple restaurants outside the gates, or stay longer and go **hiking**. Half a dozen monks live in the cells and run the place. Open 08:30–18:30 in winter, until sunset or later in summer.

Sveta Bogoroditsa (Virgin Mary) Church in the centre of the courtyard is the heart of the monastery and a five-domed masterpiece of **religious Revival architecture**. The walls of the arched outdoor gallery are richly decorated with scenes from the Old Testament, folkloric legends and imaginatively rendered scenes from Purgatory (each sin is carefully defined in Old Bulgarian). Inside, the large, intricately carved, gilded walnut-wood iconostasis stands out among a wealth of icons and frescoes depicting all manner of Biblican scenes, saints and *ktitors* (donors) who helped the monastery. Many artists laboured to create this visual symphony, including the legendary **Zahari Zograf**.

The Museum in the eastern wing contains interesting relics from the life of the monastery. Look for the **Rila Cross**, a giant, intricately carved wooden cross packed with Biblical scenes and human figures. It cost the eyes of the carver-monk Raphael who lost his sight after working on it for 12 years from 1790 to 1802. Here is the original gate of the vanished Hrelyuva Church, old firearms from the monastery's rougher days, the monastery's charter signed by Tsar Ivan Shishman in 1378, and a collection of icons gifted to the museum from around the country. Note the rare portraits of the remarkable Zograf family of painters. Open 08:30–16:30.

Below: *The Blue Bar in Borovets ski resort.*

BOROVETS

Situated at the foot of Rila's Mount Musala, pine-clad Borovets is a purpose-built **ski resort** several notches below Bansko and around 1300m (4265ft) above sea level. It was Bulgaria's first-ever resort, circa 1896, when the mayor of nearby Samokov built a wooden hut here for his tubercular wife. There are good ski facilities and a busy winter nightlife, and it is also good for **hiking** in the summer when the place becomes blissfully deserted. The gondola is open all year. There is no reason to visit unless you are skiing or hiking.

Above: *Pirin Mountains are popular for hiking and skiing.*

GOVEDARTSI

This peaceful, picturesque village some 15km (9.5 miles) west of Borovets on the Cherni Iskâr River is a good base for **hiking** trips in the summer using marked trails. There are several guesthouses and restaurants and it's a much homelier place to set up camp than Borovets. In the nearby ski resort of **Malyovitsa**, there are facilities and guides for **rock climbing**, **kayaking** or **rafting**.

BLAGOEVGRAD

Literally meaning 'the town of Blagoev', Bulgaria's first high-profile Communist in the early 1900s, **Pirin's regional centre** sports monolithic buildings from the Communist era. But it sits in a very picturesque spot and is worth a short visit on your way to Bansko or Melnik. The charmingly restored **Varosha old town** district houses some artisan workshops, art galleries and a church. The hordes of young people populating the streets are students at Bulgaria's American University and give Blagoevgrad its youthful, dynamic spirit. There are good restaurants and trendy cafés in the town centre.

BANSKO

Deservedly one of Bulgaria's top destinations, Bansko is a picturesque old town of a fiercely independent spirit, set against Pirin's glorious backdrop. Its Revival-period stone-base houses are made like small fortresses, with built-in escape routes leading out in the event of marauder or Turkish attacks. Legend has it that no Ottoman survived the night here. Bansko's heyday was during the National Revival in 18th–19th centuries, when local merchants exported cotton, tobacco and wine to Europe via the

Aegean. Bansko had flourishing schools for **icon-painters** and **wood-carvers**, whose work can be seen in the **Sveta Troitsa Church**, **Velyanova Kashta** and **Permanent Icon Exhibition**. Voted by the *Financial Times* 'the best ski resort in Eastern Europe', Bansko is indeed a top-notch **ski resort**, but also a good base for **hiking** in the Pirin in summer. The town has a cluster of attractions in the cobbled **old town**, and many characterful **taverns**. Notice that the old women of Bansko still wear long braids and dress in the characteristic woven aprons made from dyed wool.

Sveta Troitsa Church ★★★

This spectacular church from 1835 is rich in frescoes, icons and woodcarving, all created by masters of the Bansko school. It is two-storied, an unusual church feature for the Revival period, and was allegedly the biggest church built under the Ottomans. The **clock tower**, symbol of Bansko, was built later, in the 1860s, by local masters. Open daily 07:30–18:30.

Neofit Rilski House Museum ★

Next to the Sveta Troitsa Church is the house where Neofit Rilski, a national educator and monk, was brought up. His father was a teacher, hence the writing sandpits in the school-room. The house is worth seeing as a typical Bansko dwelling: the walls in places are 1.20m (4ft) thick, and it is startling to see the basic conditions in which even educated families lived. The doorways are low, in order for the visitor to bow respectfully before the host. Open 09:00–12:00 and 14:00–17:00 daily.

> ### BANSKO KAPAMA
>
> Your stay in Bansko would be incomplete without the tasty regional specialty *kapama*: pork, poultry, rice and sauerkraut slow-baked in an earthen dish. It is best enjoyed with a bottle of local wine.

Below: *Bansko is a town in southwestern Bulgaria, located at the foot of Mount Pirin.*

Velyanov's House ★★

This is an example of a wealthier Bansko house from the **Revival period**. Its name comes from its most famous owner, the master-painter Velyan, who married Neofit Rilski's sister and apparently decorated the outside house-wall with blue phoenixes as a symbol of their love. The 'blue room' is particularly attractive and a glimpse into the naïve world-view of a well-travelled, early 19th-century Bansko painter. Note the small portrait of the artist himself, wearing Napoleonic garb. The combined kitchen and bedroom is 'the mirror room': in the absence of real mirrors, the artist painted them for his wife. Open Mon–Fri 09:00–12:00 and 14:00–17:00.

Permanent Icon Exhibition ★★

The Bansko school of icon-painters took part in the decoration of **Rila Monastery**, and some of their impressive icons are on display here. Open 09:00–12:00 and 14:00–17:00, Mon–Fri.

DOBÂRSKO

About 17km (10.5 miles) north of Bansko is the tiny picturesque village of Dobârsko (literally 'the kind place'). It is set at the foot of Rila Mountain, but considered part of the Pirin district, with splendid two-way views to Pirin and the Western Rodopi. It's a good base for **hiking** in the Rila, **horse-riding**, **fishing** and **mushroom picking** in an authentic rural setting.

Church of St Theodor Tiron and St Theodor Stratilat ★★

Built in 1614, partially underground in keeping with Ottoman restrictions, this UNESCO-protected church contains rich and startling medieval frescoes. Among a number of medieval Bulgarian rulers, figures from the canon, and saints specializing in soothing the mentally ill Christ is depicted ascending in what to some people looks like a spacecraft, one of only four such representations in Bulgaria. The 'space-bubble' is in fact an Eastern Orthodox representation of an aura of light, known in the canon as Tibor light.

SANDANSKI

Sandanski is known for two things: for allegedly being the **birthplace of Spartacus**, the gladiator-leader of the greatest slave rebellion in Roman times, and for its **mineral springs** and pure air popular with those who have lung ailments. For the visitor, there is little to do here except promenade with the locals and the visiting Greeks from across the border along the long pedestrian mall, Makedonia, leading into a large town park. It is livelier and much less touristy than Melnik, and a chance to see a genuine provincial Bulgarian town.

MELNIK

Picturesquely huddled along the Melnishka River in the southwestern slopes of Pirin at the foot of giant **sand rocks**, Melnik has the endearing title of 'Bulgaria's smallest town'. Dramatically downsized from more glorious times, the town had two periods of efflorescence. In the 12th century, it was a flourishing, fortified **medieval province** under the rule of Despot Slav. Most of today's houses were built during the National Revival of 18th–19th centuries, with money from local and regional trading: wineries, viticulture and textiles. The good times came to an end when Melnik, together with Bansko, was prevented from joining independent Bulgaria and remained under Ottoman rule until the Balkan War of 1912. Passing armies sacked the town, which is why it's the smallest in the country – from 2,000 inhabitants, 500 are left. The melancholy ruins of Despot Slav's 13th-century fortress, **Bolyarska Kashta**, overlook the wild river banks at the end of town where hundreds of houses were burned. **St Nicola Church**, dating from the Revival period in 1756, stands on remains from Despot Slav's time.

REAL ESTATE

Real estate is big business in Bansko. Be aware, however, that the construction mania gripping Bansko is endangering Pirin's ecosystem, causing deforestation and turning this town into a gilded ghetto. Think carefully if and how you want to be part of this.

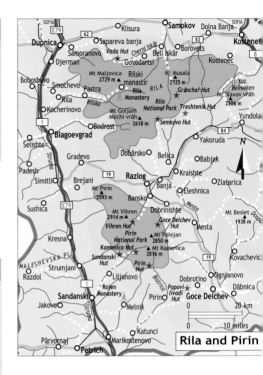

Rila and Pirin

DOBÂRSKO LEGENDS

Legend has it that Dobârsko was founded by the returning blinded soldiers of Tsar Samuil after their defeat in 1014 by Byzantine Emperor Basil, dubbed Bulgarochtonos, Bulgar-slayer. He had the 15,000 prisoners blinded, leaving a one-eyed soldier per every ten to lead them home. They headed for Rila Monastery but stopped in what is today Dobârsko to wash their eye-wounds in a healing spring. Some stayed, and so did the spring, today found in the churchyard of St Theodor Tiron and St Theodor Stratilat. The rest made it back and caused their Tsar to die of heartbreak. Other unusual village residents were the blind troubadours whose brotherhood existed here well into the 20th century and who apparently sang in a blend of Bulgarian, Greek, Gypsy and Vlach.

Although you can see the town in a couple of hours, it is a lovely spot to hang out a day or two, taste the **local wine** and walk around the *mels*, the sand-rock formations which rise vertically above the town and give it its name.

Kordopulova Kashta ★★★

Built in 1754 by the wealthy wine-merchant Kordopulos, this house is an architectural masterpiece from the National Revival period and the largest in the country from that time. Kordopulos produced wine in the extensive cellars, and traded it in wooden barrels and goats' skins to Western Europe via Salonika. The rooms are decorated in a hotch-potch of styles imported from Venice and Constantinople. The twelve Venetian and Oriental stained-glass windows overlook Bulgarian rugs in the sitting room. Each room has its designated use, and there is a 'prison' where unruly servants and sons were sent, and a 'hiding cupboard' for eavesdropping on visitors. The blue bedroom is in typical Turkish style. The rooftop terrace has a sundial-shaped mosaic. The cellar, 200m (219yd) long, contained up to 300 tons of wine at the peak of Kordopulos' trade. Now it's a pleasant winery overseen by the artistically rendered portrait of Despot Slav and his wife. Outside, the ruins of the family church, burnt down in 1912 by passing Turkish armies who also killed the last Kordopulos descendant, is a typical Melnik memento mori. Open daily 08:00–21:00.

Rojen Monastery ★★★

Picturesquely perched above the sand-rocks, 6km (4 miles) northeast of Melnik, the sexagonal Monastery stands on the ruins of a previous, 1217 monastery which was destroyed, rebuilt in the 16th century, and again partly destroyed by the Turks. The large surviving church 'Virgin Mary' dates from between 1732 and the late 18th century. Its most striking feature is the richly carved, gilded main iconostasis shining in a wall of icons, as well as the additional altar in the chapel. Particularly striking among the frescoes are the bold, lifelike images of warrior-saints. Note Saint Christopher, the travellers' protector, featured with a sheep's head. Open daily 08:00–18:30 (or till dark).

Above: *A beautiful icon in Rojen Monastery.*

Hiking in Pirin

Pirin has spectacular and rewarding hikes. There are about 30 marked trails and as many huts (*hizha*). You will need a map if you go hiking without a guide, but trails are well marked and well populated so getting lost is difficult. Recommended hikes are Sandanski to the beautiful Popina Laka area, Bansko to Hizha Vihren and Bansko to Hizha Banderitsa. The easiest is the four-hour Hizha Vihren to the Five Lakes (take a bus to Hizha Vihren). There are many day hikes or half-day hikes from Bansko, and the starting point is reached by bus from Bansko. On the trek to Vihren peak, note Bulgaria's oldest coniferous tree, the 1300-year-old *Baikusheva mura*.

Rila and Pirin at a Glance

BEST TIMES TO VISIT

Winter is the ski season in Rila and Pirin and ski resorts like Bansko and Borovets are packed. Outside the ski season, it is much quieter. Temperatures can go above 30°C (86°F), with occasional rainfall in April/May and October. June and September are the best months for hiking. Sandanski is known for its pleasant, mild climate throughout the year.

GETTING THERE

The E79 motorway from Sofia to Greece turns off to Rila Monastery and Bansko, and takes you straight down to Sandanski, with a 12km (7-mile) turnoff to Melnik. If driving into Melnik, park at the edge of the village and walk on. There are frequent buses to Sandanski, but the Melnik connection is less regular. Check the Sofia Central Bus Station for departure times. There are several Sofia-Blagoevgrad-Bansko buses daily. Almost every travel agency in Sofia organizes day trips to Rila Monastery. If driving, avoid third-class roads as they are in a sorry state. One way to get to Rojen Monastery is by organized tour from Bansko or Sofia. Better still, walk the signposted 6.5km (4-mile) track from the Bolyarska Kashta in Melnik.

WHERE TO STAY

Borovets is essentially a hotel ghetto: accommodation ranges from socialist-style monoliths to ostentatious palaces and smaller hotels. Govedartsi has family-run guesthouses. In Blagoevgrad, stay or eat at the lovely Hotel-Restaurant Christo in the green Varosha, Komitrov St, tel: (073) 880-444. Dobârsko has simple B&B rooms, some offering organic food.

Rila Monastery

There is no luxury hotel on the monastery grounds, but the listed hotels are quite adequate.

BUDGET/MID-RANGE

For the ultimate monastic experience, **Rila Monastery** offers basic en-suite rooms in the eastern wing (reception on ground floor, ask for Father Varlan). No reservations, it's on a first-come, first-served basis and often full in the summer. Ask for the newer rooms.

Tsarev Vrâh, Rila Monastery, tel: (0705) 42106. Outside the southern wing of the Monastery, panoramic views, 54 comfortable, basic en-suite rooms. Sauna, restaurant, winery and BBQ summer garden.

Pchelina B&B and Restaurant, Rila Monastery (on main road to Monastery), tel: (0888) 393-058 or (0889) 405-401. Attractive family-run B&B with patio garden for breakfast and dinner. Bulgarian cuisine and fresh trout. Walking distance from the Monastery.

Melnik

Melnik hotels are in handsome, 19th-century-style houses. Mid-range hotels are outstanding value. Where no address is supplied, simply follow the signs along the main street by the river. Most hotels and taverns have their own wineries.

MID-RANGE

Hotel Bolyarka, Melnishki Dol, tel: (07437) 383 or (07437) 368, www.bolyarka.hit.bg The low prices belie the stylish singles, doubles and apartments. Breakfast included. Sauna, mini-bar, garden restaurant.

St Nicola Hotel, tel: (0743) 7286 or 087 667836, www.qualityhotel-bg.com Perched above the main street, best views in town. Newly refurbished rooms, stylish and comfortable. Room service, breakfast included. The apartment suite is huge, with kitchen and panoramic view.

Hotel Despot Slav, tel: (07437) 248. Well-appointed rooms and apartments, breakfast included. Restaurant menu includes game.

BUDGET

Hotel Mario, tel: (052) 691-268, www.hotel-mario.melnik1.com Unmissable as you enter town. Simple rooms by the river, good traditional *mehana*.

Bansko

Bansko is cluttered with

swanky new hotels catering for skiers. There are dozens of hotels in town and near the ski facilities. Outside the winter season you'll be spoiled for choice. Even modest hotels provide transport to the ski-lifts and help with organized tours.

LUXURY

Kempinski Hotel Grand Arena, 96 Pirin St, tel: (07443) 888-8, www.kempinski-bansko.com Bansko's only five-star hotel.
Hotel Pirin, 68 Tsar Simeon, tel: (07443) 805-1, www.hotel pirin.bansko.bg Modern four-star hotel in the heart of Bansko with sauna, gym, pool. Other luxury options are **Tanne**, 7 Georgy Nastev, tel: (07443) 810-0, www.hotel-tanne.com, and the cosier **Glazne**, 2 Panayot Hitov, tel: (07443) 902-2, www.glazne.bansko.bg Both have panoramic views.

MID-RANGE

Elitsa, 12 Gotse Delchev, tel: (07443) 839-1, www.hotel-elitsa.com Modern décor, very central.
Elena, 3 Vassil Drumev, tel: (07443) 825-4. Convenient, panoramic, own restaurant and bar, sauna, gym.

BUDGET

Alpin, 6 Neofit Rilski St, tel: (07443) 807-5, www.alpin.bansko.bg Great value en-suite rooms with cosy local-style décor, in the old town. The mehana serves

local food. Sauna, transport to chair lift, ski hire.
Villa Crystal, 24 Hristo Matov, tel: (07443) 236-4, www.vila-crystal.com Central, lovely garden.

It is practically impossible to eat badly in the Pirin region: the regional cuisine is delectable and the restaurants countless. Blagoevgrad and Sandanski have some good restaurants in the centre. Melnik and Bansko burst with traditional *mehanas*, all of which serve grilled meat (signposted as 'BBQ') and local delicacies like Bansko *kapama* and Melnik *kavarma*. Most taverns have menus in English. Ask if there is a non-smoking area.

Rila Monastery

There are two simple taverns at the East gates of the Monastery. *See* hotels for more.

Bansko

Bansko has an abundance of *mehanas*, many with live folk music. **Dedo Pene**, 1 Bujnov St, tel: (07443) 8348, www.dedopene.com is the oldest *mehana* in town, circa 1820. **Bakanova Mehana**, in the main square; big range of dishes, excellent pizzas. **Kasapinova Kashta**, 4 Yane Sandanski, off Vazrajdane Sq; excellent Bulgarian food in 19th-century décor.

Melnik

Mehana Mencheva Kashta,

tel: (07437) 339, www.melnik-mehana.com In a 200-year-old house. Folk décor complete with stuffed animal heads.

There are souvenir shops all over Melnik and Bansko. Bansko is known for its crafts: icons, woven rugs, pottery, carved wood, bags and socks. Souvenir shops can be found around the main square, or buy the real deal from local women.

Spatia Tours at 2 Slaveikov Sq, Sofia, tel/fax: (02) 986-1212, http://wildlife.spatia-tour.com Specialize in wildlife and mountain tourism. Pony riding from Litova Kashta at the far end of Melnik. **Emilyana Holidays**, Neofit Rilski 28, tel: (07443) 250-0, Bansko, offer guided tours of Bansko and day tours to Rila Monastery, Melnik, Rojen Monastery, Kovatche-vitsa, and a bear reserve. Tourist Information Centre in Nikola Vaptsarov Sq.

Balkan Holidays Services, Sofia-based travel agent specializing in Bansko, tel: (02) 989-6263, office@balkan holidaysint.com **Altam Real Estate Agency**, 5 Vâzrajdane Square, tel: (07443) 6401, www.altam-realestates. com offer self-contained apartments for short-term hire.

4
Plovdiv
and the Rodopi

At the crossroads between Europe and Asia Minor along the banks of Bulgaria's biggest river, Maritsa, Plovdiv is the country's second biggest city (population 380,000) and a key place in the historical region of Bulgarian Thrace. Plovdiv is one of the oldest cities in Europe – older than Athens and Rome – and, unsurprisingly, it sits on top of many layers of civilization. Attractions include ancient ruins and the Old Town's handsome 19th-century National Revival architecture. Nearby sights are Bachkovo Monastery, the second largest in the country, the medieval Asenova Fortress and the Thracian site of Perperikon. Although dandyish, old-worldly Plovdiv and the rural, timeless Rodopi offer contrasting experiences, Plovdiv is a convenient gateway to the Rodopi.

Named after a Thracian divinity, the Rodopi is the oldest mountain range in the Balkans and a dramatic land to boot. Prehistoric peoples and later Thracian tribes lived here, and this is the birthplace of legendary singer Orpheus. Seen from the highest points of the road from Plovdiv, the Rodopi Mountains look like a sea of dark mounds. Despite their moderate relief (average elevation is around 800m/2625ft), the Rodopi are shaped by spectacular karst formations and deep river canyons, and boast several major natural sights, including caves and gorges. The ski resorts Pamporovo and Chepelare are bustling in winter, while spots like the regional centre Smolyan or villages like Shiroka Lâka attract summer hikers. The people of the Rodopi are known for their gentleness and sense of beauty, and, in true Orphic tradition, their haunting music. There is a large Muslim population here –

DON'T MISS

★★★ Plovdiv's Old Town: one of Europe's oldest towns, exquisite Revival architecture, atmospheric cobbled lanes.
★★★ Plovdiv's Roman Amphitheatre: a preserved theatre from Emperor Trajan's time.
★★★ Bachkovo Monastery: scenic mountain setting, murals.
★★★ Yagodina, Uhlovitsa and Devil's Throat Caves: ancient caves in the Rodopi Mountain.
★★★ Smolyan's Historical Museum: a showcase of Rodopi culture and ethos.
★★★ The Rodopi songs: hear some of the most haunting music on the Balkans.

Opposite: *View of the Rodopi Mountains.*

CLIMATE

Plovdiv has a Mediterranean-influenced climate, with hot, dry summers (Jun–Sep), mild winters and a wet spring (Apr–May). The Rodopi Mountains combine Mediterranean breezes from the south and cold northern air. The result is warm summers, mild spring and autumn, and heavy snow in winter, with temperatures as low as −15°C (5°F). Unless you come to ski, the best time to visit is late spring (May) and summer.

both ethnic Turks and Bulgarians – and in most villages you will spot their mosques and colourful dress.

PLOVDIV

Ancient people 6000 years ago spotted the fertile plains of Lower Thrace, and what is today Plovdiv has been invaded, rebuilt and renamed ever since. It first rose as Eumolpias, a

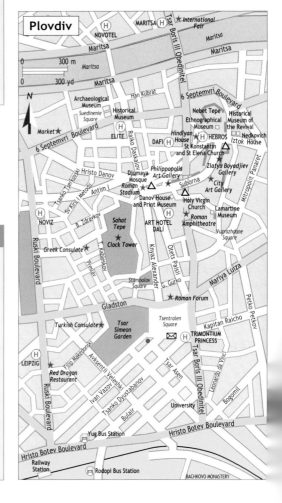

ONCE A CITY

Plovdiv is the birthplace of urban culture in Bulgaria. Though today Old Plovdiv is a museum to its glorious 19th-century self, people here take pride in the fact that this was a sophisticated urban centre while Sofia was still an Ottoman backwater. Plovdiv has always been a progressive city and an important hub for the democratic movement in the 1980s. Many talented Bulgarians come from Plovdiv: jazz musician Milcho Leviev, footballer Hristo Stoichkov, Olympic champion Stefka Kostadinova and writer Angel Vagenstein.

fortified settlement around three *tepes* or hills – Nebet, Taksim and Djambaz – taking the name of its founder, the mythical Thracian King Eumolpes, son of the gods Hemus and Rodopa. In 342BC Philip of Macedon took the town, built some more walls and renamed it after himself, Philippopolis. The Romans gave the town a new life in the 1st century AD by building the biggest military road in the Balkans, Via Militaris, and making it the capital of Roman Thrace, Trimontium, 'the town on the three hills'. With the decline of Rome, Trimontium endured Hun

Above: *The busy streets of Plovdiv, one of the oldest cities in Europe.*

and Goth depredations, and was rebuilt by Byzantine Emperor Justinian in the 6th century (he referred to it as 'my Rome'). When the Slavs arrived, they called it Puldin, and eventually, after changing hands between the Bulgarians and the Byzantines, the town became part of the First Bulgarian Kingdom. The Ottomans defaced the city when they arrived in the 14th century, but it rose from its ashes again, this time as Philibe, and eventually became a cultural centre of the National Revival in the 18th and 19th centuries. This period created Plovdiv's enchanting town architecture and gave the cobbled lanes of the Old Town their unique atmosphere. Several of Plovdiv's attractions are house museums. The listed sights can be used as a sightseeing route, starting in Djumaya Square.

Roman Stadium ★

Under the statue of Philip II of Macedon, beneath the bustling Djumaya Square, part of a Roman Stadium has been excavated. Although you can only see it from street

HOUSE MUSEUMS

There are several other interesting house museums worth visiting. Danov House, perched on Taksim Tepe, belonged to a cultural pioneer and Bulgaria's first publisher; an early printing press is on display. Balabanov House, built in the early 19th century by Hadji Panayot Lampsha, a merchant and money lender, features a *hayet* (reception room) and carved ceilings. French writer Alphonse de Lamartine never lived in Lamartine's House, but he did stay for three days in 1833 and the name stuck, such was Plovdiv's yearning to feel closer to Europe. The exhibits are of little interest, but the house is a masterpiece of Revival architecture. Note the foundations following the natural slope and the jutting stories maximizing the space inside.

level, the seats are clearly defined. It is uncertain whether the stadium was built during Philippopolis or Trimontium, but it is certain that some 30,000 people could be seated here during the Apollonian and Alexandrian games.

Djumaya Mosque ★★

Built in the 1400s under Sultan Murad II in place of the demolished Orthodox Church St Petka, this is one of the largest and oldest surviving mosques on the Balkans. Interestingly, its architecture shows the influence of Byzantine and old Bulgarian building styles. The rich blue decoration, however, is typically Islamic – plant motifs, quotations from the Q'uran – and probably dates from the late 1800s. Although the casual side entrance next door to the Oriental Patisserie suggests disuse, the mosque is active, so remove your shoes before you enter. Open every day.

Holy Virgin Church (Sveta Bogoroditsa) ★★

Although a church, and later a monastery, has existed on this site since 9th century, it was partly destroyed by the Ottomans when Plovdiv fell in 1371. In the Revival era in 1844, a new church was erected under the protection of two progressive local brothers. In 1859, services were delivered in Bulgarian, marking the beginnings of a hard-won independent Bulgarian church. Many of Plovdiv's pro-independence metropolitans are buried here. They are depicted in the hallway, together with scenes from Bulgarian history.

Roman Amphitheatre ★★★

Walk up from Sveta Bogoroditsa and through the court-yard of the Music School, and Plovdiv's most stunning sight will greet you. This is Trimontium's theatre, and one of the world's best-preserved ancient amphitheatres. It dates from the reign of Emperor Trajan in the 2nd century, and could seat between 5000 and 7000 spectators. It perches over Plovdiv's busiest road and fits with the Old Town's natural shape, while offering a panoramic view to the 'new' town. Despite a devastating earthquake in the

4th century which destroyed its stage, it has been expertly reassembled, statues and all. It is used for performances in the summer. Gates close at 18:00 but you can get a reasonable view from the outside.

Above: *Roman Amphitheatre, Plovdiv.*

City Art Gallery ★★

This intriguing collection by top Bulgarian artists traces the development of Bulgarian fine art in the century from the inception of the first State School for the Fine Arts in Plovdiv to the 1990s. The beautiful classical building (1881) is a former girls' college. The collection includes household names like Konstantin Velichkov, Georgi Evstatiev, Ivan Mrkvichka who taught at the School, Sirak Skitnik, Bulgaria's first impressionist, Dechko Uzunov, Zlatyu Boyadjiev, and Vladimir Dimitrov Maistora, the doyen of Bulgarian peasant portraiture. The first Bulgarian secular painting is here – a portrait of revered educator Sofronii Vrachanski by an unnamed artist from Tryavna. Tryavna was known for its icon-painting school, and the transition from iconography to portraiture is clear. Explanations in English. Open 09:00–12:00 and 13:00–17:30, closed Sunday.

PLOVDIV FAIRS AND FESTIVALS

Plovdiv lives up to its cultural traditions with a wealth of festivals: the Festival of Orchestral Music in January, the Opera and Chamber Music Festival in June, Trakiisko Lyato Festival of Music in August, the Puppet Festival in September, the International Film Festival in Oct–Nov. The international Plovdiv Trade Fair dates from 1892 and is the biggest in southeast Europe. It fills hotels and streets in May and September – good times to see the fair itself, but not so good for seeing the town.

Zlatyu Boyadjiev Gallery ★★★

Zlatyu Boyadjiev (1903–76) is one of Bulgaria's greatest artists and this is the biggest collection of his work. You can see the two periods of the artist's work, before and after the illness which paralysed his right side. He painted with the left hand thereafter, and the difference in styles is clear. His evocative, ironic, and disturbing portrayals of Bulgarian life throw light on the national psyche. Famous works to look out for: self-portrait with his wife, the epic *Two Weddings* and *Orpheus*, and his otherworldly pastoral canvases. Open 09:00–12:00 and 13:00–18:00 daily in summer; 08:30–12:00 and 12:30–17:00, closed weekends, in winter.

St Konstantin and St Elena Church ★★

In the spot where this richly decorated church stands today, there was an early Christian temple to the 38 Plovdiv martyrs executed under Emperor Diocletian in 304. An icon depicting the martyrs takes pride of place inside the church entrance (right-hand side). Later, the temple was dedicated to the apostles Konstantin and Elena. In the 1830s, with the permission of the sultanate, two churches – St Konstantin and St Elena, and St Nedelya

Right: Orpheus, *by Zlatyu Boyadjiev, one of Bulgaria's greatest artists.*

up the road, in shabby condition) – were built simultaneously. The icons around the iconostasis are the work of the country's best icon-painters, including Stanislav Dospevski and the prolific Zahari Zograf. The gilded 'Viennese-style' iconostasis and all the murals were the work of two artists. Open 09:00–18:00 (08:00–19:00 Friday and Sunday). The icon museum next door is worth perusing: it contains 15th- to 19th-century icons by famous masters from Plovdiv and southern Bulgaria.

Historical Museum of the Revival ★

This is one of Plovdiv's three historical museums (the others are the Print Museum in Danov's House and the Archaeological Museum, currently closed) and the most interesting if you wish to understand Bulgaria's most dramatic recent epoch. The museum, housed in a splendid Revival house, focuses on the history of Plovdiv under the Ottomans, and the National Revival period of the 1800s. Open 10:00–18:00 summer, 09:00–17:00 winter, Sat and Sun 10:00–17:00.

Ethnographical Museum ★★

This collection offers a fascinating glimpse into the life and customs of the Thracian Plains and Rodopi region – regional wear, huge cattle bells, rugs, trades – and the house itself is one of the most stately survivors of the town's heyday. It belonged to Plovdiv tradesman Argir Koyumdjioglu and was built at his behest in 1847 by a Rodopean architect. Open 09:00–12:00 and 14:00–17:00 every day.

Nedkovich House ★★

This 1863 home is one of the classical-style European houses in the Old Town, and was the property of wealthy textile trader and city doyen Nikola Nedkovich. Of special interest are the murals of world cities, the sunburst carved ceilings, and the authentic furnishings and possessions from the Nedkovich household (including the double 'lovebirds' chair' which was meant for the daughter and her fiancé, but she never married). Note the downstairs

Above: *National Revivalist architecture, Balabanov House, Plovdiv.*

BACHKOVO MONASTERY MURALS

Zahari Zograf painted the imaginative *Last Judgement* mural of the Church of St Nikolai (built 1836) in the smaller courtyard. Unusually, he painted a self-portrait with two other artists in the upper left corner, while the Turks and sinners to the right are on their way to hell. The refectory has stunningly colourful murals: scenes from the life of Jesus, and a constellation of philosophers from antiquity mixed in with the saints, all painted by an anonymous artist/artists in the 1600s. Note the date 1601 carved on the marble table.

'gossip room' (*klyukarnik*) looking out onto the street. Open 09:00–17:00, closed Sat and Sun.

Nebet Tepe ★

Nebet Tepe is one of the Old Town's romantic lookout points where you can literally stand on top of the city's multi-layered past. This history-packed hilltop contains ruins from the 7th-century BC Thracian settlement Eumolpias; the later citadel of the Hellenic period; the extensions from Emperor Justinian in 6th century, which included an underground passage leading to Maritsa River; and remains from medieval defensive add-ons, mostly water tanks built at the time of the Second Bulgarian Kingdom in 13th–14th centuries. Unless you are an archaeologist, it's hard to tell which stones date from when, so just soak in the centuries beneath your feet.

Hindlyan House ★★★

If you only see one house museum, this should be it. It is not only the most richly decorated, but also the best showcase of Eastern and Western fusion, a masterpiece inside and out. It was built from 1835–40 for Stepan Hindlyan, yet another wealthy tradesman. Note the beautiful naivistic murals of world cities like Alexandria, Istanbul, Venice and Stockholm, the little marble *cheshma* (water fountain) in the reception room which ran with rose water, the Oriental-style marble bathroom with Roman-style under-floor heating, and the fortified stone tower in the courtyard which was the family's treasury. Open 09:00–17:00.

AROUND PLOVDIV
Asenova Krepost ★

Perched high above the road from Plovdiv to Smolyan, 2km (1.2 miles) south of Asenovgrad, is the Asenov Fortress, an early 13th-century remnant from the reign of Tsar Ivan Asen II. It was used by Bulgarian tsars until their Kingdom fell under the Ottomans. The symbol of the fortress is the only fully restored building, the tower-like 12th-century Church of the Holy Virgin of Petrich, which

Above: *Bachkovo Monastery, Bulgaria's second largest monastery.*

s now a functioning church. Access is by car, or ask the bus driver to drop you off, then walk up from the road to a glorious vista of Plovdiv and the Thracian Plain.

Bachkovo Monastery ★★★

Some 30km (20 miles) south of Plovdiv, strategically and scenically placed at the gateway to the Rodopi on the road to Smolyan, is Bulgaria's second largest monastery after Rila. It has had a busy history: founded in 1083 by two Georgian aristocrats in the Byzantine army, a religious hub in the Second Bulgarian Empire (12th–14th centuries), destroyed by the Turks, rebuilt in the 17th century, painted by the prodigious Zahari Zograf in the 1840s, and served as exile and resting place of 14th-century luminary Patriarch Evtimii whose marble sarcophagus is outside the Archangel Church. The giant Diasperus Lotus tree in the courtyard was brought from Georgia two centuries ago.

There are three churches on the monastery grounds. The biggest, the Church of the Assumption of Our Lady, was built in the 16th century and is unusually large for the time. Ties with the Greek Episcopy and the

HIKING IN THE RODOPI

The Rodopi Mountains, like Rila, are a paradise for hikers, with their grassy slopes, flowers and unspoilt forests. Shiroka Lâka is a good base for shorter hikes, and so are Smolyan, Pamporovo and Chepelare from where you can hike to Shiroka Lâka and back in a day.

ORPHISM

Mystery surrounds the fascinating Orphic cult practised in Perperikon and across Thrace from around the 9th century BC. It is considered a toned-down variation of the Dionysian cult, though its fertility-worshipping practices were not exactly ascetic: Bacchanalian dances, mimicking of dismemberment (as in Orpheus's and Dionysius's deaths), sacrifices of animals and humans, and orgies.
We can only guess what the Dionysians did when they really let their hair down. Orphism was philosophically influential and references to its key concepts are found even in Plato, i.e. the idea of the body as a prison of the soul.

monastery's special status within the Ottoman province permitted its construction. Special features are the price less 1310 silver icon of the Virgin brought from Georgia, the 17th-century iconostases, and the bold 19th-century murals. The chuch adheres to the much smaller 12th-century Church of the Archangel, whose open arched gallery contains the work of Zahari Zograf (1850). Open 07:00–19:00, winter 07:00–18:00.

Perperikon ★★★

Located 95km (59 miles) from Smolyan and 100km (62 miles) from Plovdiv, the rock-hewn ancient city of Perperikon is a detour, but considering that it's a new archaeological sensation (discovered in 2000), it's well worth it. Perperikon was the centre of a sprawling Thracian settlement in the Rodopi, and the hub of cult activities dating as far back as 3000BC. Later, thanks to its Dionysian priests (Dionysius was known in Thrace as Zagreus), it became to the Thracians what Delphi was to the ancient Greeks. In the 1st–4th centuries AD, the conquering Romans built temples, palaces and an Acropolis, and Perperikon reached its apogee as a pagan centre before it was sacked by the Barbarians. The arrival of

the Bulgars and later the Byzantines kept it in good shape, until it was once again sacked by the Ottomans in the 14th century.

You need some imagination to conjure the ancient glory of these stones, but as you go up the massive stone staircase, you feel the strong energy of the place, and the views are glorious. Look out for the altar, sacrificial pits, stone wine presses (wine and fire were used by oracles), royal sarcophagi, and Byzantine and medieval remains. There is no entry fee or guide, but maps in English are available and recommended. Some 2km (1.2 miles) from Perperikon are the labyrinthine ancient gold and silver mines, but it's easy to get lost inside them without a guide. A summer solstice Festival of the Arts is held here in June.

Above: *Statue to Orpheus and Eurydice, Smolyan.*
Opposite: *Footsteps in stone, Perperikon.*

SMOLYAN

Smolyan is the Rodopi's regional centre and Bulgaria's longest town, at 10km (6 miles). Winding along the Cherna (Black) River and up the hills, it reveals breathtaking views of the Rodopi, which compensate for the equally breathtaking ugliness of its 1970s architecture. A statue of Orpheus with a lyre and his beloved Eurydice stands in the centre, and the old district has preserved its handsome 19th-century houses. The town was destroyed in the 17th century during a violent Islamizing campaign against the Rodopi population. The converted survivors rebuilt what is now the central part of the town, and the Turks called the new village Pashmaklu. Later, after the Liberation, it was renamed Smolyan, after a Slavic tribe. Smolyan is a pleasant, laid-back provincial town with several interesting attractions, and a good base for exploring the natural wonders of the region. It offers good tourist facilities.

RODOPI WINTER SPORTS

The Rodopi's top winter sports resort is the purpose-built Pamporovo – big, expensive, often booked out, and fairly impersonal despite the stunning surroundings. There is a good range of ski runs and cross-country trails, the snow boarding is excellent, and facilities are very good. The more downmarket and far more charming villages of Chepelare, Shiroka Lâka and Momchilovtsi are an alternative base if you have transport. Chepelare also has two excellent ski-runs of its own.

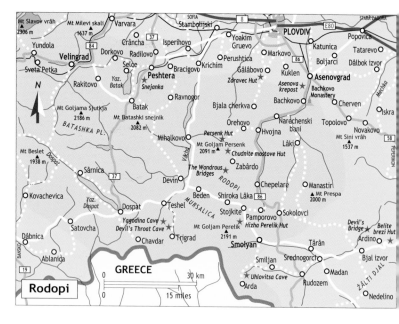

Rodopi

Historical Museum ★★★

Reached via some stone steps across from Hotel Smolyan, this outstanding museum offers a fascinating glimpse into the history and ethos of the Rodopi region, starting with Stone Age findings. Particularly interesting is the ethnographic section which displays the typical multicoloured rugs and costumes. Giant cattle bells, elaborate heavy jewellery, life-like *kukeri* (ritual mummers), and examples of crafts and customs make this an unmissable collection. Open every day 09:00–12:00 and 13:00–17:30, or later on request. Tel: (0301) 627-27. Next door is the worthwhile Smolyan Art Gallery, which has a large 20th-century collection by local and foreign artists connected with the Rodopi. Open 08:30–12:00 and 13:00–17:30, closed Monday.

Planetarium ★★

Smolyan seems an unlikely place to see the stars through a telescope, but this is Bulgaria's biggest planetarium and well worth a visit. A minimum of three people must turn up for the daily foreign-language session at 14:00, or you pay the full fee (which won't break the bank). You need to call beforehand to request a tour in your language. Tel: (0301) 830-74. Closed Sunday.

THE RODOPI
The Devil's Bridge ★★★

This spectacular, perfectly symmetrical three-arched bridge, dating back to the 16th–17th centuries, is worth the rough drive; 25km (15 miles) northeast of Smolyan, along a rough road crisscrossing the Arda River canyon. Various dark legends surround the bridge, including the ubiquitous folkloric story of a person's shadow being built-in, in this case the builder's wife. Others says that the reflection of Satan himself can be seen from the 11.5m (38ft) high bridge. Whatever you see, the fact remains that the bridge was built by the Ottomans to carry their caravans from Plovdiv to Ksanti in Greece.

The Wondrous Bridges ★★★

On the road from Plovdiv to Smolyan, a turn-off to the right will take you to these truly wondrous stone formations. The giant 'bridges' were caused by an earthquake in which a cave collapsed and was subsequently carved out over the millennia by a river. Sit in the nearby chalet with a cup of herbal tea and marvel.

Uhlovitsa Cave ★★

Some 25km (15 miles) south of Smolyan and accessible only by car, this cave is known as an underground palace. It features four abysses and beautiful 'waterfall' formations. Open 09:00–17:00, closed Monday, Tuesday and during winter.

Below: *Bagpipe music is popular in the Rodopi.*

Above: *A river entering Devil's Throat Cave.*

The Devil's Throat Cave ★★★

Passing through the awesome Trigrad Gorge on the way to Trigrad, you will see the entrance to the Devil's Throat. As you enter this abyss-cave, the roaring noise of the river waterfalls carving the rocks and the deadly chill of the marble-stone quickly explain the cave's name. Known also as the 'Gate to Hades' or 'Orpheus's Cave', where Orpheus entered the Underworld to look for Eurydice, this is a place of darkness. In 1970 two divers died during an expedition here, and all exploration of the cave ceased thereafter. The cave is 400m (1312ft) long, and one of very few accessible caves in a region boasting 200. The highest waterfall which flows into it is 42m (138ft) high, and although you can hear it, only part of it is visible from the viewing platform. It is believed that the Thracians who lived in the area threw their dead chieftains' bodies into the river, and since the cave acts as a giant filter so that nothing leaves it except water, the bodies presumably remained inside. Open summer 08:00–18:00, winter on request. Tel: (0304) 220; 0889163238.

Yagodina Cave ★★★

This magnificent, 10km (6-mile) long cave was inhabited by eneolithic people, traces of whose existence can be seen inside the natural entrance to the cave, 1km (0.6 mile) up the road from the official entrance. The entertaining, informative tour passes through many spectacular halls and lasts about 50 intense minutes. The cave was open to visitors only 25 years ago, and exploration continues. You will see giant, curtain-like stalactites and stalagmites, the so-called 'leopard-skin rocks', bizarrely shaped rock formations, 'cave-pearls', and if you go in summer, the cave's only inhabitants – bats. Open during summer 09:00–16:00, lunch break 12:00–13:00, tours begin every hour. Open in winter on request. Tel: (0304) 19 or (0304) 200.

Shiroka Lâka ★★

More than just a village, Shiroka Lâka is a protected ethnographic and architectural reserve. Set on the banks of the Shirokolâshka River, this pretty village is distinguished by its ancient bridges and typically Rodopean stone houses with small windows, high chimneys and hidden trapdoors. They were built like fortresses, to withstand Turkish attacks. The village was populated in the 17th century by Christian survivors of Ottoman attacks in the region. During the violent 18th and 19th centuries, it was a stalwart of national consciousness in a largely Islamized area. At the annual Shiroka Lâka Bagpipe Festival in July, the region's best bagpipe players showcase their mastery. The Sveta Bogodoritsa Church was built in 1834 in only 38 days, painted by the famous brother-artists Zahari and Dimitâr Zograf, and immediately used as a school. There is not much to do here except wander around the steep, cobbled lanes and admire the houses, but this is also an alternative base to Smolyan for hiking and exploring the region.

> ### KUKERI FESTIVAL
>
> The first week of March is a good time to be in Shiroka Lâka. The traditional exchange of *martenitsi* (red and white tassels to mark the coming of spring) on 1 March is followed by celebrations on 3 March, Independence Day, but the cherry on the cake is the hugely colourful Kukeri Festival, held on the first weekend of March. This pagan fest of fertility and exorcism is kept alive in other parts of Bulgaria and celebrated on different dates. Mummers adorned with cattle bells dance in woollen costumes and furs, topped by bizarre animal masks and headdresses.

Below: *Quaint houses in Shiroka Lâka.*

Plovdiv and the Rodopi at a Glance

BEST TIMES TO VISIT

Plovdiv is hot and swamped by tourists in high summer. Best times to visit are late spring (end of May) and early summer (June) or early autumn (September). The Rodopi can get hot in July to August, but late spring, summer and early autumn are good times to visit. Winter is a good idea only for winter sports. Early spring (March and April) has unpredictable weather – rain or snow – and chilly nights.

GETTING THERE

Plovdiv is an hour and a half by car or two hours by bus on the E80 motorway from Sofia. There is an hourly bus from Sofia's Central Bus Station. There are also several daily trains from Sofia's Central Railway Station. Plovdiv's Train Station and both Bus Stations (Yug and Rodopi) are next to each other in the southern part of town, 15 minutes from the centre on foot. Buses to Chepelare, Pamporovo, Smolyan (2 hours), and Bachkovo Monastery leave from the Rodopi station. Most other buses leave from the Yug station. Going from Plovdiv to Perperikon via Kârdjali is a much better option than going Smolyan-Perperikon. There are six daily buses from Sofia's Central Bus Station to Smolyan. From Smolyan, there is a bus back to Plovdiv every hour 07:00 to 18:00

from the bus station, or every hour 09:00 to 16:00 from Hotel Smolyan. Several daily buses go from Smolyan to Shiroka Lâka. Access to the caves is easiest by car. There are four daily buses from Smolyan to Sofia.

GETTING AROUND

Plovdiv's Old Town can only be seen on foot, and the town itself is small enough to get around on foot. Otherwise you can use taxis outside the Old Town.
Roads in the Rodopi can be tricky in the winter, so if driving, you must have winter tyres. In early spring the snow thaws, so both the weather and the roads are unpredictable. In Smolyan, use taxis or your feet.

WHERE TO STAY

Plovdiv is relatively expensive. Most hotels are outside the Old Town. There are no budget hotels in the Old Town beyond two youth hostels and private rooms.

Plovdiv
LUXURY
Hotel Hebros, ul. Konstantin Stoilov 51A, Old Town, tel: (032) 260-180, fax: (032) 260-252, hebrosh@ tourism.bg Plovdiv's most exquisite hotel and one of Bulgaria's best. Ten rooms in gorgeously restored 200-year-old house. Charming garden and facilities for meetings. Award-winning Hebros

Restaurant has a refined European menu.
Trimontium Princess, 85euro/110euro, apartments. Renovated since socialist times. www.trimontium-princess.com
Hotel Maritsa, Tsar Boris III Obedinitel 42, just across the Maritsa River and next to the Plovdiv Fairgrounds, tel/fax: (032) 952-727. Large four-star hotel with casino and restaurant. Discounts for groups of six or more. Foyer and deluxe rooms in decadent faux-rococo style.

MID-RANGE
Art Hotel Dali, Otets Paisii 11, tel: (032) 621-530. Tastefully decorated hotel in a quiet street near Djumaya Sq. Breakfast, bar, Internet, one suite with a 'Turkish bath'.
Hotel Dafi, Benkovski 23, tel: (032) 620-041, fax: (032) 629-434, www.hoteldafi.com Stylish 21-room three-star hotel beside Djumaya Sq. Bar, breakfast, Internet, jacuzzi in suites.

BUDGET
Hotel Elite, R. Daskalov 53, tel: (032) 624-537. Comfortable family hotel, 10 minutes from Djumaya Sq. Despite the busy corner, rooms are insulated.

Pamporovo
LUXURY
Hotel Orlovets, tel: (03021) 846-9. Five-star hotel with views and classy restaurant.

Plovdiv and the Rodopi at a Glance

Special rates for groups.
Hotel Murgavets, tel: (03021)
831-0. Popular restaurant
Bulgarian Village downstairs.

MID-RANGE/BUDGET
Hotel Zora, tel: (03021) 812-0.
Three-star, sauna, restaurant,
good value. Check for
organized Rodopi tours
in summer.

Smolyan
MID-RANGE
Hotel Plaza, 69 Bulgaria St,
tel: (0301) 637-67. Central,
comfortable family hotel.
Parking, sauna and a good
restaurant.

BUDGET
Kashtatas Trite Eli (House of
the Three Firtrees), 1
Srednogorets St, tel: (0301)
642-81. Cosy family hotel,
great views from top floor,
buffet breakfast. Hostess
offers guided tours and car
hire.

Shiroka Lâka
There are several family
hotels. **Kalina** and **Margarita**
along the main street offer a
similar homely standard.
Kalina has a decent restaurant.

Trigrad
For the ultimate in rural
tourism and good access to
caves and hiking, base your-
self in Trigrad village. A good
family hotel is **Silivryak**, tel:
(3040) 220, at the top of a
shocking village road. It has a
taverna and kitchen for

guests. The owners organize
local tours, horse-riding and
cave visits.

WHERE TO EAT

Plovdiv
Chevermeto, 15 Otets Paisii
St, tel: (032) 626-137. Stylish
restaurant offering *cheverme*
(spit-roast lamb) and other
Rodopi specialties, fine wines
and live music.
Trifon Zarezan Winery, 16
Otets Paisii St, across from
Chevermeto. Cheerful, cosy,
cheap taverna and winery.
Mehana Dayana, Dondukov
St. Popular, noisy taverna. If
you want to see locals having
fun, this is the place.
Oriental Patisserie, next to
Djumaya Mosque. Cakes and
patisseries, freshly squeezed
juice. Non-smoking hall.

Plovdiv Old Town
The Old Town has many
restaurants in restored houses.
Restaurant Puldin, 3 Knyaz
Tsertelev St, tel: (032) 631-
720. In a former Dervish
monastery from the Persian
Order of the Whirling
Dervishes. Built on top of the
original Roman city walls.
Excellent menu and live
classical music.
Restaurant Kambanata, 2
Sâborna St, tel: (032) 260-
665. Terraced layout, fine
dining, retro music.
Restaurant Hebros (*see*
hotels)
Grajdanski Club, 1 Stoyan
Chalukov St, tel: (032) 624-
139. Cheap, popular hang-

out, good Bulgarian food and
grills, summer garden.

Smolyan
Mehana Mechta,
Al. Konstantinov, tel: (0301)
633-53. Traditional *mehana*,
use car or taxi.

SHOPPING

Plovdiv's Old Town has some
good souvenir shops. In the
Rodopi, there are street stalls
and small shops in towns and
villages. Honey lovers, look out
for the dark Manov honey sold
at the Plovdiv market. A typical
Rodopi gift would be a hand-
woven woollen blanket or rug.

TOURS AND EXCURSIONS

Karlâk Smolyan, tel: (0301)
626-88 or 0898642083,
organize specialized tours
and cave visits.
Horse Riding, Trigrad,
tel: 0886018578.

USEFUL CONTACTS

Plovdiv, unbelievably, does not
have a tourist centre yet, but
Hotel Trimontium has some
information. **Rent A Car**
Plovdiv or Sofia, tel: (036) 162-
109. **Rodopi bus station**,
Plovdiv, tel: (032) 6970-607.
**Tourist Information Centre
Smolyan**, Bulgaria 5, tel: (0301)
625-30. They offer a thorough
booklet on Smolyan and the
area. **Smolyan bus station**, tel:
(0301) 631-04. Tourist
**Information Centre Shiroka
Lâka**, 48 Kapitan Petko
Voivoda St, tel: (03030) 233,
www.shirokalaka.com

5
Central Bulgaria

Central Bulgaria is dominated by two mountains: the lower Sredna Gora and the partially Alpine **Stara Planina**, locally called simply 'Balkan' (the origin of the Balkan Peninsula's name). Stretching 550km (341 miles) from Serbia and Montenegro. to the Black Sea and ranking third in altitude (the highest peak is Botev at 2376m/7795ft), Stara Planina – the Old Mountain, a misnomer given its relatively young relief – is the geographical backbone of the country. One travel writer referred to it as 'the most Bulgarian of mountains', true in the sense that the region was the hotbed of freedom fighters in the 18th–19th centuries and became the scene of the fiercest battles in the **Russian-Turkish war** for the liberation of Bulgaria. It is also the home of **Veliko Târnovo**, seat of medieval Bulgaria's tsars; architecturally picturesque towns like **Koprivshtitsa** and **Tryavna**; ethnographic complexes like **Etâra** and **Arbanasi**; and breathtaking **monasteries** like **Troyan**, **Dryanovo** and **Preobrajenski**. To the northeast, the **Shumen Fortress** and the former royal capital of **Veliki Preslav** offer a glimpse into the Golden Era of Bulgaria's Middle Ages.

But the region's history does not begin with the Middle Ages. Prehistoric people left a **Neolithic dwelling** in Stara Zagora, and archaeologists keep digging up **Thracian gold treasures and tombs** in the plains of Kazanlâk, traditionally known as the **Valley of Roses** and now dubbed the **Valley of the Thracian kings**. **Roman ruins and mosaics** lie under the streets of **Stara Zagora**, and much of the Roman wall at spa-town **Hissarya** still stands.

DON'T MISS

★★★ **Koprivshtitsa:** exquisite Revival architecture in a historical town.
★★★ **Veliko Târnovo:** the majestic medieval Tsars' city, Tsarevets, and the scenic cobbled lanes of the old town.
★★★ **Troyan Monastery:** third largest in the country.
★★★ **Etâra:** ethnographic complex in lovely mountain setting.
★★★ **Tryavna:** scenic mountain setting and beautiful Revival houses, home of the Tryavna woodcarving school.
★★★ **Shumen Fortress:** medieval remains of hilltop Tsars' fortress with stunning views.

Opposite: *Fortress walls, Tsarevets.*

KOPRIVSHTITSA

The ultimate tongue-twister for anybody learning Bulgarian, Koprivshtitsa is otherwise a convenient 110km (68 miles) east of Sofia, 1050m (3444ft) up in Sredna Gora, and a popular weekend trip for city dwellers. This not surprising, since a walk in the crisp mountain air and among the cobbled lanes takes you into another time when wealthy merchants lived in handsome houses. Here in 1876, the first gun of the **April Uprising** went off, on bridge since called 'The first gunshot', and this is also the birthplace of Revival luminaries – the Uprising's leaders Benkonvski and Kableshkov, belletrists Luben and Petko Karavelov and poet Dimcho Debelyanov. In the bloody aftermath of the rebellion, Koprivshtitsa, unlike many other villages, was spared by the Turks, thanks to the local elite who literally bought it off. Its characteristic period houses are colourful and creative; many are house museums, and some are 300 years old.

Oslekov House ★★★

The owner of this sumptuous 1850s house with a triple arched entrance was the rich merchant Oslekov. His trips abroad are reflected in the murals of cities, the wood carvings and objects from around the world. The canon i

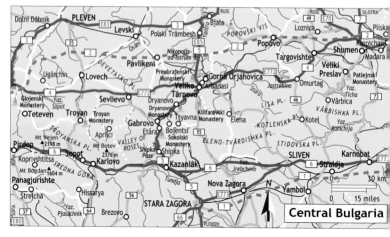

Central Bulgaria

SHOPPING IN CENTRAL BULGARIA

You can find Koprivshtitsa felt rugs, cloths and bags in the small workshops along Debelyanov St. Rose oil and rose products can be bought in Kazanlâk Museum of Roses. Woodcarvings and other quality crafts are on sale in Tryavna's souvenir and antique shops. In Veliko Târnovo, Rakovska St and the lanes around Samovodska Charshiya Complex have great souvenir shops and galleries.

Left: *Lyutov House, built in 1854, was owned by a travelling milk merchant.*

he courtyard is, however, local and it was used in the April Uprising where Oslekov was killed. Open 09:00–17:30, or 17:00 in winter, closed Monday.

Lyutov House ★★★

The owner, milk merchant Lyutov, had this house built by craftsmen from Plovdiv in 1854, and painted the wall cityscapes himself as a memento of his travels. Each room is painted a different colour, and downstairs is an attractive display of **felt rugs** made in the unique Koprivshtitsa style. Open 09:30–17:30, or 17:00 in winter, closed Tuesday.

Uspenie Bogorodichno/Church of the Assumption ★★

The pretty blue exterior and hilltop views of this 1817 church just off Dimcho Debelyanov Street are more interesting than its typical interior. In the gardens is the grave of Kableshkov, the Plovdiv- and Istanbul-educated 25-year-old revolutionary who set off that first fatal gun and committed suicide in captivity only two months later. His birth house on Kableshkov Street is a museum to the Uprising.

Debelyanov House ★

Dimcho Debelyanov was a gifted lyrical poet who died

THE FIRST GUNS

Koprivshtitsa is the home of the ill-fated April Uprising of 1876. The Uprising, fomented for many years by a secret revolutionary committee, suffered fatally from a lack of coordination. The first guns were fired by impatient hotheads while the rest of the country was not ready. This was the rebellion's downfall, and entire villages went down with it. The reprisal massacres were so terrible (*see* Batak panel, page 63) that they incurred 'civilized' Europe's outrage and helped ignite the **Russian-Turkish war** which liberated Bulgaria two years later.

aged 28 in World War I. This creaky house is typical of middle-class Koprivshtitsa, and contains his books, an audio recording of his poems, and family belongings. The statue in the garden is of his anxiously waiting mother.

Troyan Monastery ★★★

The third largest in the country and the largest in Stara Planina, this attractive and popular monasterial complex has an eventful history. Established in the 17th century by a hermit, oft-destroyed by the Turks, and controlled for a time by the Greek eparchy, it flourished at the time of the **National Revival** when it hid revolutionaries, stashed arms, and had no less than 80 monks involved in the central revolutionary committee. During the **Russian Turkish war**, it was converted into a field hospital for Russian soldiers, cared for by the monks.

Although the complex contains buildings from different eras, like Rila Monastery, the overall impression is one of harmony. The **Church of the Assumption** has lavish frescoes by the ubiquitous 19th-century master painter **Zahari Zograf**, an exquisite walnut-carved iconostasis, the work of Tryavna carvers, and a curious icon of the Three-handed Holy Virgin which has been here from the inception of the monastery and was possibly a gift from a visiting monk from Mount Athos. Among the Zograf frescoes, note the portraits of the 27 monks who lived here at the time, the self-portrait with the abbot and, in the courtyard, the lion and elephant mural symbolizing the people's strength and patience under Ottoman rule.

Hissarya/Hissar

There are two reasons to visit Hissar – the 22 **mineral springs** and the **Roman ruins**. The springs are why the Romans came in the first place, named their town Diocletianopolis after Emperor Diocletian, and built walls in the 4th century to protect their medicinal spas. The walls along the main road and the park, originally 2315m (2532yd) long, are remarkably well preserved, and the massive 3m (10ft) thick gates are particularly impressive. Go for a leisurely walk through the pleasantly restored town and fragrant gardens – the only thing to do in between spa sessions. These you can have either at the Mineral Baths in town or the specialist Hissar and Augusta hotels, where you can have anything from detox to underwater massage and mud treatment.

Starosel Thracian Tomb ★★

Starosel literally means 'old settlement', and this is no lie. The sensational Thracian tomb uncovered in 2000, some 10km (6 miles) from the village of Starosel or 30km (20 miles) from Hissar, dates from the late 5th century BC. It is the biggest Thracian tomb in Europe – 20m (65ft) high and 90m (295ft) in diameter – and is believed to have contained the remains of **King Sitalkes I**, the powerful ruler of a first united Thracian kingdom which invaded neighbouring Macedonia. In a nearby mound, archaeologists found substantial treasures of gold and silver jewellery, horse appliqués and armoury. The two-chamber tomb, reached via a massive stone staircase, is supported by Doric columns and features a coloured stone frieze. More discoveries are bound to be made, but not until someone funds the archaeological work. Guided tour in Bulgarian only. Open 09:00–17:30.

THRACIAN TOMBS

Thracian civilization remains largely a mystery, despite the recent sensational discoveries of the sanctuary of Perperikon and more tombs. Many of the thousands of Thracian tombs on Bulgarian territory have been plundered over the centuries (some, like Helvetia, as early as Roman times). Some, however, have yielded dazzling treasures, on display in Sofia's History and Archaeology Museums and Kazanlâk's Museum. For ancient history buffs, a **guided tour** of the visitable tombs is recommended due to bad roads and infrastructure (see At a Glance, page 93). Around Shipka in Central Bulgaria, seven tombs have been found, of which the best are **Sarafova Mogila**, **Helvetia** and **Golyama Kosmatka** (the tomb of King Seuth III). **Sveshtari** in the northeast is unique for its stunning carved and painted murals (see page 120).

Left: *The impressive Roman ruins at Hissar.*

THE BULGARIAN ROSE

The *Rosa damascena* of Kazanlâk is responsible for producing the traditional Bulgarian **rose oil** used in perfumery and also referred to as 'liquid gold' because of its price. The rose was probably brought from Tunisia by a wealthy Turk in the 17th century. The rose oil of Kazanlâk – the world's best – makes up 80% of world production. The rose harvest lasts for 30 days each year and involves some 2000 pairs of hands. In order to produce just 1kg (2.2lb) of rose oil, for which 1300 blossoms are hand-picked and steam-distilled. The entertaining **Rose Festival** in the Valley of Roses (30 May and 1 June) features a 'Rose Queen' contest, a rose parade and ritual rose harvesting.

Opposite: *Gold mask of Thracian King Teres.*
Below: *Valley of the Roses.*

KAZANLÂK

Sitting in the picturesque valley between the Stara Planina and Sredna Gora ranges, Kazanlâk is the regional centre of the Rose Valley, itself the geographical centre of Bulgaria. Kazanlâk is unremarkable, but worth a detour for the two local attractions: **roses** and **Thracian treasures and tombs**.

Museum of Roses ★

You can only see rose harvesting in May, but the rest of the year this museum 2.5km (1.5 miles) north of town is a good substitute. You can see how rose oil is distilled and buy rose products from the museum shop. The museum was under renovation at the time of writing. Take a taxi from town. Open 09:30–17:00, winter on request.

Kulata Ethnographic Complex ★

This complex is rather grandly named considering it is a couple of handsome period houses built by Tryavna masters and showcasing the transition from village to town lifestyle in the Kazanlâk region. It was owned by Hadji Eno, a rose oil merchant. If you don't have time for the Rose Museum, make an appointment here and the Kulata caretakers will demonstrate the process of rose water distillation with authentic equipment, with a tasting of rose jam and tea. Located at the bottom of Tyulbe Park on the way to the tomb. Open 09:00–17:00, closed in winter.

Kazanlâk Thracian Tomb ★★

The original 4th–3rd-century tomb, first discovered by soldiers in 1944, can't be viewed for preservation reasons, but an exact replica stands next door, at the top of Tyulbe Park. The small beehive-type tomb is remarkable for its uniquely colourful dynamic frieze depicting scenes of a funerary feast, chariots and warriors – the only fully preserved Hellenistic frieze in Bulgaria. The tomb was built for a Thracian ruler, here depicted with his wife at the feast in a poignant parting scene. Open 09:00–18:00, winter on request.

Iskra Historical Museum and Art Gallery ★★★

The ancient and artistic treasures housed in the tomb-like, monolithic building at the north end of Sevtopolis Square beat the rose oil as Kazanlâk's highlight. **The Museum** contains the region's rich history, from prehistoric findings to medieval and Ottoman artefacts. But the highlight is the recently found Thracian treasures from nearby tombs: the imperious solid **gold mask of King Teres** (the original is in Sofia's Archaeological Museum), the life-like bronze head of **King Seuth III**, and an exquisite royal **gold wreath**, part of a 73-piece treasure.

The Gallery contains valuable paintings by **Bulgarian artists** from the 20th century, including Dechko Uzunov, Vladimir Dimitrov-Maistora, and Tsanko Lavrenov's Plovdiv cityscapes. In the worthwhile **collection of icons**, look out for the rare icon of 'The Virgin holding a rose'. Open 09:00–17:30.

MONASTERIES OF THE BALKAN RANGES

If hilltop monasteries are your thing, Stara Planina is your place. Here are some of the more interesting monasteries in the region: **Glojenski Monastery** off the Sofia-Varna road at Yablanitsa was founded in the 13th century by Ukrainian Prince Gloj and subsequently rebuilt many times. The beautiful **Cherepishki Monastery** perched atop the Iskar Gorge off the Sofia-Mezdra road was built in the 14th century and rebuilt in the 16th, and has sheltered many writers and revolutionaries. **Klissurski Monastery** off the Sofia-Montana road, built in the 13th century, offers comfortable rooms in a lush setting. The small but perfectly formed **Sokolski Monastery** (1832), off the Kazanlâk-Veliko Târnovo road, offers stunning views and frescoes, rooms for the night, and a *mehana* nearby. Note the eight-spouted fountain in the courtyard, built in 1868 by famed architect Kolyu Ficheto.

STARA ZAGORA

Stara Zagora, a city of linden-lined streets, is a pleasant town in the southern hills of Sredna Gora worth at least half a day's visit. Its regular 21st-century look conceals two surprising facts: that it is 8000 years old, and that it was razed to the ground by Suleiman Pasha's army in 1877 – he mistook a Bulgarian detachment of volunteers for General Gurko's forces and, realizing his mistake, took it out on the city. A third fact is easier to trace today: this was the prosperous **Augusta Trayana**, a Roman city named after Emperor Trajan, which cut its own coins and was linked to Constantinople by a major road. The City Garden in the centre is particularly lovely in spring.

Neolithic Dwellings ★

Walk down Knyaz Boris I St west of the City Gardens towards the hospital, and you will find **Europe's oldest preserved dwelling**, dating from 6000BC. Housed in a specially constructed building, the two 'rooms' are full of Stone Age pottery and tools. Charred remains of wheat were found in clay vessels – the result of a prehistoric fire. English tour on request (recommended), tel: (042) 62-2109. Open Tue–Sat 09:00–12:00 and 14:00–17:00, Monday on request.

Roman Ruins ★★

The Roman remains of Stara Zagora are scattered. Northwest of the City Garden, in St Mitropolit Metodi Kusev St, are the impressive columns and steps of the **Ancient Forum**, currently overrun by weeds. The **Roman**

Right: *The remote architectural village of Bojentsi.*

Thermae (mid-2nd century AD) are west of the Neolithic dwellings; the visit must be organized with a guide. On the ground floor of the Post Office in St Knyaz Boris I St east of the Gardens, you can see the surviving **floor mosaic** of a 4–6th-century AD residence: the images represent the seasonal cycle of life. The most impressive survivor is the floor mosaic of a 4th-century reception room in St General Stoletov St, the only mosaic of its kind in Bulgaria. The images of animals and Nereids are accompanied by inscriptions in old Greek: 'Welcome' and 'Cheers'. To visit, call the Historical Museum, tel: (042) 62-931.

The Historical Museum
Closed at the time of writing but will display Thracian and Roman artefacts when it reopens in late 2007. Open 09:00–12:00 and 13:00–17:00.

Above: *An icon artist at work in Etâra.*

Bojentsi ★★
Huddled in the heart of central Stara Planina at the end of a vertiginous road 750m (2.4ft) above sea level, the **architectural village** Bojentsi looks much as it did two centuries ago. The village is **600 years old** and, because of its reserve status, untouched by modern construction. The Revival houses built by 18th- and 19th-century merchants and craftsmen typically have a stone base, whitewashed façades, protruding eaves and slated roofs. Only 40 souls live here, but it is a popular retreat for artists and writers, and a good base (in spring and summer) for short hikes, strolling the steep cobbled lanes and enjoying the pure mountain air and lush setting.

Etâra ★★★
Just off the scenic E85 road, 8km (5 miles) from Gabrovo, Etâra **ethnographic village complex** gives you a glimpse into the ethos of pre-modern Bulgaria. The village is set amid lush hills along a river, and the architecturally preserved Revival houses contain **workshops** where craftspeople showcase and sell traditional **crafts**: tannery, jewellery, woodcarving, and weaving on hand-looms. This is the place to buy souvenirs and snack on old-fashioned pastries. Open 09:00–18:00, day ticket.

> **KABILE**
>
> Kabile Archaeological Reserve is some 20km (12.5 miles) off the Sofia-Burgas road, past Stara Zagora. Though poorly maintained and sporadically open, Kabile is a joy to history buffs. This was the hilltop site of a major Thracian town-sanctuary from 2000BC until Roman times. It minted its own coins with images of Artemis, the revered goddess here, and maintained close relations with the now submerged Seuthopolis. After devastation by the Goths, Byzantines and Bulgars took over. The Roman and medieval ruins are substantial, and the on-site museum contains valuable artefacts. Open 08:00–20:00, winter 10:00–16:00. Reached by car or bus from Yambol. Contact Yambol Historical Museum for visits, tel: (046) 66-2736.

Right: *Dryanovo Monastery.*

Dryanovo Monastery ★★

This whitewashed, eye-pleasing monastery conveniently situated on the Gabrovo-Veliko Târnovo road has had a long and dramatic history. Only the original 17th-century church remains after repeated destruction by the Turks; in the outer walls of the church you can see bullet holes from the latest, most comprehensive destruction by fire in the 1876 April Uprising. Nearly all the defender-revolutionaries at the church perished, including legendary leaders Bacho Kiro and Priest Hariton. The dramatic cliffs and lush greenery are the visit's highlight, and so is the short, scenic walk to the nearby prehistoric **Bacho Kiro Cave** (guided tour, open 08:00–19:00, winter 10:00–16:00). The **Dryanovo eco-trail** is four hours long and starts and finishes at the monastery (*see* At a Glance, page 93). Comfortable accommodation available. Open every day.

TRYAVNA

With its old stone bridges, singing clock tower and beautiful period houses, Tryavna is a one of Stara Planina's **highlights**. The Revival houses in dark wood were built by craftsmen and masons from the **Tryavna school**, and the ground floors served as their workshops. If you stay overnight (and you should), listen for the quaint old 'town song' played by the clock at 22:00. Its lyrics are by native Pencho Slaveikov, one of Bulgaria's finest classical writers. The loveliest cobbled street in town bears his name.

Shkoloto ★

Housed in one of the country's first secular schools circa 1930s, this eccentric museum is several tiny museums in one, all reflecting local life: a collection of old clocks; paintings by local artist-brothers in a curious 'neo-ethno-graphic' modernist style; and a collection of Tryavna school icons and paintings. Open 09:00–18:00, winter 10:00–17:00.

Daskalov House ★★★

This handsome house belonged to silk merchant Daskalov. Its two architects were local woodcarvers, and the two spectacular **carved suns** on adjacent room ceilings were the fruits of a six-month-long competition between them in 1808: the older carver created a more 'mature' sun, the younger a 'brighter' one – spot which is which. Bulgaria's only **Museum of Woodcarving** is here, with examples of the Tryavna school. There is also a 'patriotic room' with carved heads of kings and Revival luminaries. Open daily 09:00–19:00, and in winter 09:00–17:00.

Left: *A picturesque house in Tryavna.*

THE TRYAVNA SCHOOL

The Tryavna school of wood-carving reached its heyday during the National Revival. Its fame spread as far as Persia, and local masters were commissioned by wealthy home-owners in the Balkans to decorate their houses. Many of Bulgaria's churches and monasteries were decorated in the Tryavna style (*see* Troyan Monastery, page 78). Flower motifs and suns were central to this style – perhaps the influence of Islamic religious art. Classes at the art school can be arranged through Shkoloto and the tourist office.

HIKING IN THE BALKAN RANGES

Stara Planina is ideal for hiking. It offers the seriously fit one of the longest mountain treks in the Balkans – from Kom Peak on the Serbian border to Emine Peak on the Black Sea – which takes 20–25 days. Here are some less ambitious hikes from places mentioned in this chapter: Dryanovo Monastery eco-trail (4 hours), Etâra-Sokolski Monastery (1 hour), Shipka Pass (3–4 hours), Shipka Monastery-Shipka Monument (2 hours).

Above: *Houses in Veliko Târnovo cling to the steep ground along the Yantra River.*

Museum of Icons ★★

The number two icon museum after the Alexander Nevski Crypt in Sofia, this handsome collection contains about 180 fascinating Tryavna school icons from the 17–19th centuries. Follow signs to the top of the hill on the other side of the train line. Open 08:00–16:00, winter 09:00–18:00.

VELIKO TÂRNOVO

The green City of the Tsars, with its awesome ruined **medieval fortress Tsarevets** and houses clinging to the steep banks of the snaking **Yantra River**, is simply unmissable. Târnovgrad, as it was known until modern times, was the seat of rebellion against the Byzantines who ended the First Bulgarian Kingdom in 1014 (*see* pages 12–13). The leaders of the successful revolt were the brothers Petâr and Asen, who became rulers of the **Second Bulgarian Kingdom** (1185–1393), and who today have a virile Socialist monument in the Asenovtsi Park across the river, next to the Art Museum. Two centuries of efflorescence ended with the Ottoman invasion, in which Tsarevets was destroyed, along with the town's life. Things didn't pick up until the early 19th century with the National Revival, and here, in 1879, the Constitution of an independent Bulgaria was penned.

The highlight of your visit is of course the fortress, but leave a day for the rest too. Climbing the cobbled streets of the **old Revival district Varusha** rewards you with spectacular views. The **Samovodska Charshiya**, the 19th-century marketplace behind Rakovski Street, was the hub

of prosperous Târnovgrad's commercial life where tradesmen and artisans converged. Traditional **workshops** and
galleries recreate the convivial atmosphere and keep the
quiet old streets alive today, and there are a couple of
interesting museums. Go wandering to the west of
Tsarevets in **Asenova quarter**, where the merchants lived,
and check out the remarkable murals of the **Forty Martyrs'
Church**, **St Peter** and **St Paul**, **St Georgi** and **St Dimitâr**.

Tsarevets ★★★

The remains you'll see after you pass through the three gates
are the work of several civilizations and eras. The first traces
of Thracian settlements here date back 4000 years, but it
was the Byzantines who built a fortress in the 5th–7th
centuries, followed by the early Slavs and Bulgars in the
8–10th centuries, then again the Byzantines when they
invaded, and finally, the Second Kingdom of the Asen
brothers rose on top of those ruins. Four hundred houses and
shops were excavated here, but only their foundations
remain. Take a left along the fortress wall and walk among
the remains of some **22 medieval basilicas and churches** in
the western part of the complex, to the furthest point: a 13th-
century **monastery** and **Execution Rock** from where
undesirables were pushed off. Continue past a *bolyar's*
home (nobleman) and to the memento mori of the **Tsar's**

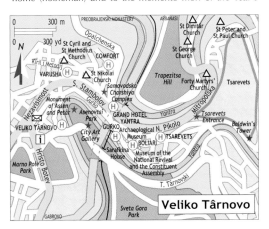

Veliko Târnovo

ASEN AND PETÂR

Asen and Petâr, brother *boyars*
from Târnovo, sought favour
from the Byzantine Emperor
Isaac-Angel in 1185, and were
booted out unceremoniously.
Upon returning home, they
started fomenting a revolt. This
was facilitated by the capture
of Byzantium's second city,
Thessaloniki, by the King of
Naples. Asen and Petâr, with
true political flair, announced
that the patron saint of
Thessaloniki, St Dimitâr, had
fled his conquered city and
arrived in Bulgaria, 'proven'
by the apparition of a miraculous St Dimitâr icon in
Târnovo. They had a church
built and consecrated in the
name of the saint, and this is
where they announced that
Byzantium no longer ruled
these lands – an ambitious
statement which came true a
year later. You can see the
church, the town's oldest, in
the Asenova district.

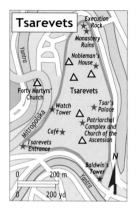

Palace from where some 20 tsars ruled and where only a wall and fragments of tiled floors remain. Roman columns were found here, either from a previous Roman construction or from Nikopolis-ad-Istrum up the road. At the top of the hill, the **Patriarchal Complex** offers a glorious view, somewhat offset by the bleak modernist images of the artist who, in 1985, filled the **Church of the Ascension** with his vision of medieval Bulgaria. From here, walk down the hill and take a left along the eastern wall, to **Baldwin's Tower** and yet more breathtaking views. Take care at Baldwin's Tower and desist from climbing if you're unsure about heights. Try to catch the fabulous night-time **sound and light show** which really brings the fortress to life, but happens without notice – ask at your hotel or listen for the bells. Open 08:00–19:00, winter 09:00–17:00. Tour guides at the entrance.

Sarafkina House ★★

A wealthy banker and his wife lived in this 1861 Revival house ('sarafin' meant money-lender). The absorbing ethnographic collection throws light on urban life and customs during the Revival: folk crafts from the Târnovo school, domestic interiors, photographs from village festivals, and a colourful collection of textiles, heavy belt-buckles (*pendari*), festive breads from different regions and painted Easter eggs. Note how, seen from the street, the house has two levels, but from the riverside it has five, like most hill houses here. Located at 88 Gurko St, a street below the Archaeological Museum. Open 09:00–12:00 and 13:00–18:00, winter 09:00–17:00, closed on weekends.

Archaeological Museum ★★

Go down the stone steps from Ivan Vazov St to access this tranquil museum set in a lovely courtyard. There are artefacts from nearby Roman town Nikopolis-ad-Istrum, but the highlight are the collections from the time of the Second Bulgarian Kingdom and Târnovo's heyday: beautiful ceramics, miniatures by artists from the Târnovo school, the life-like frescoes of saints from the original medieval Preobrajenski Monastery (*see page 89*), and the coins room. Open 09:00–18:00, winter 09:00–17:00.

THE TOWER OF BALDWIN

Baldwin's Tower was allegedly the prison of the leader of the Fourth Crusade and first Latin Emperor of captured Constantinople, Baldwin I of Flanders, after his army was defeated in 1205 by **Tsar Kaloyan's** army at Adrianopolis (Odrin). Baldwin, who enjoyed emperorship for only a year, was captured and possibly housed in this tower until his execution – which appears to have been sudden and in contrast with the initial hospitality of his captor. Some say that he tried to seduce Tsar Kaloyan's wife – which might well explain the execution. It's also likely that Tsar Kaloyan was incensed by the recent capture of Philippopolis (Plovdiv) by the Franks and took it out on his hostage.

AROUND VELIKO TÂRNOVO

Preobrajenski Monastery ★★★

Perched high in the hills 7km (4.5 miles) north of Veliko Târnovo, the atmospheric Monastery of the Transfiguration is worth seeing as much for its fascinating murals as for the stunning views across the Yantra canyon. Originally built in the 14th century some 600m (656yd) away, it was destroyed by the Ottomans and entirely rebuilt in a Revival style in the early 19th century, with special permission from the Sultan. It is the work of renowned architect **Kolyu Ficheto** and the ubiquitous painter **Zahari Zograf** who spent three years on the murals. Two murals in the main **Church of the Transfiguration** are of particular interest: the *Wheel of Life* on the outer wall, depicting the emptiness of a life without piousness and virtue, and the *Last Judgement* where various sinners endure punishment (thieves, adulterers, witches, drunks, traitors). As in Rila and Bachkovo Monasteries, these are masterpieces where Balkan superstition meets Eastern Orthodox moralist dogma. The exquisite iconostasis and its icons were crafted by Tryavna carvers and painters.

ARBANASI

This pretty **architectural village reserve** is an alternative base to V.Târnovo and an idyllic spot for horse-riding, hiking and exploring nearby sights. Arbanasi was settled in the 15th century by Albanian Christians and flourished between the 16th and 18th centuries under the benevolent ownership of Sultan Suleiman's son-in-law. Local tradesmen made fortunes from trading within the vast Ottoman Empire, and five churches and two monasteries were built in that period – a sign of the town's special status. The ugly end came in the form of savage depredations by *kurdjalii* (Ottoman bandits) in the 1790s. Today, it's a popular spot for weddings and holiday houses for the new rich.

Below: *Preobrajenski Monastery contains some fascinating murals.*

Konstantsaliev House ★★★

The most impressive of the house museums, this 17th century house-fortress was restored in the 19th century and belonged to a tradesman whose offices were in Constança Romania, hence the name. If the stone base and wooden upper storey, the internal staircase, the hiding spaces and woman's quarters (spot the maternity room) seem familiar that's because they are local variations of the reinforced village house typical of both late-medieval and Revival Bulgaria – think of Bansko and Shiroka Lâka. The extensive **shop** downstairs has excellent crafts and booklets on Arbanasi. Open 09:00–18:00, winter 09:00–17:00.

Nativity Church ★★

This is the oldest of Arbanasi's five churches and, behind its drab exterior, the most richly decorated, with 3500 figures. The murals date from the 17th century and the frescoes in the narthex or antechamber were painted by one of the donors. The murals are a curious blend of Eastern Orthodox moralism and asceticism, and the European humanism of the time signalled by the images of ancient Greek philosophers, which somehow managed to penetrate as far as the Ottoman provinces.

Another church worth seeing for its rich murals is 17th century **St Archangel Michael and St Gabriel** which contains the portraits of its donor and his family. The frescoes in the antechamber were painted by artists from Thessaloniki and Bucharest. As in the Nativity Church, the iconostasis is the work of Tryavna carvers.

SHUMEN

The main reason to come here is the Shumen Fortress. The **History Museum ★★** (09:00–17:00, pleasant courtyard café) has fabulous Thracian, Roman and medieval Bulgarian artefacts from the sites below, including a model of the Shumen Fortress. The 1744 **Tombul** (plump) **Mosque ★★** is the second largest in the Balkans and Bulgaria's loveliest.

Shumen Fortress ★★★

About 3km (2 miles) up the hill from Shumen, in the north

east, is one of Bulgaria's most scenic open-air sights. The partially restored Fortress thrived during the First and Second Kingdom as a fortified town. Soon after the Ottomans invaded, it was briefly taken in 1444 by the young Polish **King Vladislaus III of Varna**, on an ill-judged crusade against the Ottomans which ended with his death at the Battle of Varna. Some of the artefacts are in the small on-site **museum**. On the way up to the fortress, you'll pass the brewery that makes the popular **Shumensko pivo** beer. Open 09:00–18:00, winter 09:00–17:00.

Above: Shumen Fortress, *one of Bulgaria's most scenic sights.*

Veliki Preslav ★

Though the scattered ruins of Great Preslav are less than great, this was the seat of one of 10th-century Europe's major empires. Hire a guide at the museum as the ruins are poorly signposted. The **Museum** is where you get a sense of the cultural efflorescence of the capital: the jewellery, mosaics and painted ceramics by Preslav artisans are particularly fine, including the famous ceramic icon of Theodor Stratilat. Open 08:00–18:00, winter 08:00–17:00 and weekends 09:00–17:00.

Madara Horseman ★

Carved into a rock 23m (75ft) above ground, this UNESCO-protected 8th-century horseman hails from the early days of the Bulgarian nation which united the populous Slavs and the nomadic Bulgars. The horseman was Khan Tervel on a march against favourite enemy Byzantium. We know this from the inscriptions, which date from three different khans/tsars in the space of 100 years. Walk up another 300 or so rock-hewn steps to the ruins of **Madara Fortress**, once part of Veliki Preslav's defense, to earn a staggering view.

> ### MONUMENT OF THE CREATORS
>
> The granite monstrosity you see across the valley from the Shumen Fortress is a monument to the Creators of the Bulgarian State. It was built for the Communist-orchestrated 1981 celebrations of Bulgaria's 1300th anniversary. Every able-bodied man in the area was enlisted to work on the project in 'volunteer brigades'. The monument, which depicts the early tsars (who had a fine eye for design and no doubt would have been appalled), actually looks better the further you are from it. If you must see it close-up, take a taxi from town or walk the scenic 3km (1.8-mile) path from Shumen Fortress.

Central Bulgaria at a Glance

Spring and summer are best. Winter is charming in villages by the fire, but you need winter tyres for the roads, and places like Bojentsi are pretty isolated.

Troyan Monastery is reached via the road to Troyan, off the E773 Sofia-Burgas highway. The turnoff to Koprivshtitsa is earlier and access is easy; daily buses from Sofia. The road to Starosel is shabby. The roads crossing Stara Planina at Shipka Pass (E85) and up to Troyan Monastery (35) are slow in the winter, so allow extra time. To reach Bojentsi, take the Donino turn-off on the E85 road from Gabrovo to Veliko Târnovo. Visit Shumen on the way from Veliko Târnovo to Varna, or as a day-trip from Varna. For Madara, Shumen Fortress and Veliki Preslav, take a taxi from Shumen. Preobrajenski Monastery, Arbanasi and Nikopolis-ad-Istrum can be reached by taxi from Veliko Târnovo.

In this region the best transport is private car or taxi. The bigger towns are easily seen on foot.

Koprivshtitsa
LUXURY/MID-RANGE
Kalina, 35 Palaveev St, tel: (07184) 20-32. Elegant period rooms in a gorgeous garden.
Trayanova Kashta, 5 Gereniloto St, near main square, tel: (07184) 30-57. Four large,

enchanting rooms. Bicycle hire and trekking info.

BUDGET
Hotel Zdravec, Belovejdov St, tel: (07184) 22-86. Simple, cosy rooms, large garden.

Troyan Monastery
Comfortable hotel rooms and eateries at the monastery, tel: (06952) 28-66, or stay in Troyan 10km (6 miles) away.

Hissarya
LUXURY/MID-RANGE
Hotel Hissar, tel: (0337) 62-781, end of ul. Gurko. Refurbished inside (but the exterior remains ugly); offers top-notch spa treatments. Two restaurants and three bars, rooftop dining.
Hotel Augusta, tel: (0337) 63-821. Five minutes from the Hissar, revamped and offering spa treatments.
Hotel Galeri, tel: (0337) 20-85, 15 Gurko St. New, smaller hotel. Mineral water only, rooms with Jacuzzi available. Massages and other treatments.

BUDGET
Victoria, tel: (0337) 65-535, Ivan Vazov St. Humble and featureless, but convenient Socialist-era hotel, across the main road from the centre.

Stara Zagora
LUXURY/MID-RANGE
Hotel Uniquato, 36 Sava Silov St, tel: (042) 66-1155. Classy boutique hotel in a restored old building in the centre. Excellent Italian cuisine, good breakfast.

Etâra
MID-RANGE/BUDGET
Hotel Stranopriemnitsa or **Traveller's Inn**, next to and overlooking the complex, tel: (066) 80-1832. Comfortable.
Hotel Perla, across the road from the village, tel: (066) 80-1984. Excellent value family hotel with large balconied rooms and a restaurant.

Bojentsi
MID-RANGE/LUXURY
Hadjivelinov Inn, tel: (088) 53-33148. www.bg-guesthouse. com Comfortable rooms fitted with antique village furniture.
Parlapanova Kâshta, tel: (067193) 229, office-s@ rholiday.net Impeccable whitewashed rooms in period house, plus bar and *mehana*. One room has a fireplace.

Tryavna
LUXURY/MID-RANGE
Zograf Inn, 1 Slaveikov St, tel: (0677) 49-70, www.tryavna.bg/ zograf The only hotel in the heart of the old town. Modern, spotless, but bland.
Ralitsa, 16 Kaleto St, tel: (0677) 22-62, www.tryavna.bg/ralitsa 15 min from main square, past Maistora Restaurant. Three-star comforts and great apartments.

Veliko Târnovo
BUDGET
Hotel Varusha, 6 Vâstanicheska St, tel: (062) 245-54, www.hotel-varusha.com Quiet rooms, best deal in town.
Hotel Comfort, 5 Tipografov St, up from Samovodska Charshia,

tel: (062) 628-728. No-frills family hotel, views of Tsarevets, but too dear for its category.

MID-RANGE
Hotel Gurko, 70 Gurko St, tel: (062) 330-46. Handsome rooms in period house by the river, great balcony views.
Hotel Boliari, 2 Ivanka Boteva St, tel: (062) 606-002, www. boliarihotel.com Two minutes from Tsarevets, balcony views, impeccable but bland, spa.

LUXURY
Grand Hotel Yantra, 2 Opal-chenska St, tel: (062) 600-607, www.yantrabg.com Four-star with Jacuzzi, spa, gym and restaurant. Good for groups.
Hotel Tsarevets, 23 Chita-lishtna St, tel: (062) 601-885, www.tsarevetshotel.com 5 min from Tsarevets. Classy boutique hotel in period building.

Arbanasi
MID-RANGE/LUXURY
Hotel Izvora, tel: (062) 60-1205, www.izvora.com An attractive hotel with winter and summer gardens, *mehana*, pool, and various activities.

WHERE TO EAT

Koprivshtitsa
Hotel Mehana Sveti Georgi, near 'The First Gunshot' bridge, tel: (07184) 23-93. Two-floor period *mehana* in a 236-year-old house. Traditional cuisine.
Restaurant 20 April, in main square, tel: (088) 93-68220. Large rooms and large portions of hearty national cuisine.

Hissarya
The restaurants and café around the town-centre park are best, otherwise dine in the hotels with other tourists.

Stara Zagora
Hotel Uniquato (*see* Where to Stay). Or try **Pizzeria Venezia**, K. Ganchev St, tel: (042) 63-8174. Pizzas, salads and Italian mains among Roman décor.

Bojentsi
Café-Hotel-Candy shop, near central square. This nameless place offers delicious sweets and pastries, Turkish coffee, yoghurt. Ideal for breakfast.

Tryavna
Maistora, 7 Kaleto St, tel: (0677) 32-40, 10-min walk from main square. The owner is one of the region's finest chefs. Eat here and you'll not want to leave town. Open 11:00-15:00, 18:00-24:00.
Starata Loza, 44 Slaveikov St, tel: (0677) 45-01, opposite Daskalov House. Traditional cuisine with a modern twist under a garden vine.

Veliko Târnovo
Shtastlivetsa, underneath Hotel Trapezitsa, ul. Stambolov 79, tel: (062) 60-3253. Hearty Balkan and European cuisine. Book a seat with a view. If you are at least two and not vegetarian, order *tsiganska tava*.
Architect's Club, 14 Velcho Djamiata St, tel: (062) 62-1451. Balkan food, nice views and a terrace; vegetarian options.

Starata Mehana, tel: (062) 63-8878. Good traditional food in the town's oldest *mehana*; folksy setting, modest prices, views from closed-off terrace.
Mecha Dupka (Bear's Den), Samovodska Charshia Square, tel: (062) 34-794. Traditional fare in a 'den' with bear skins.

TOURS AND EXCURSIONS

For cycling while sightseeing (e.g. a monastery tour), contact www.cyclingbulgaria.com For a 2-day organized experience of the Kazanlâk Rose Festival: www.rose-festival.com
Stara Zagora Historical Museum for viewing Roman remains, tel: (042) 62-931, www.chambersz.com/museum
Bacho Kiro Tourist Association for hikes, climbing and caving near Dryanovo Monastery, tel: (0676) 23-32. **Dryanovo Tourist Association Council of Tourism**, tel: (0676) 24-36.
Veliko Târnovo Tourist Info, Botev St, behind Mother Bulgaria monument, tel: (062) 62-2148. Open Mon–Fri, 09:00–12:00, 13:00–18:00.

USEFUL CONTACTS

Koprivshtitsa Info Centre, tel: (07184) 21-91, help with accommodation and trekking maps. **Kazanlâk Museum of Roses**, tel: (0431) 63-741 for appointments in winter and organized visits to Thracian tombs. **Tryavna Tourist Office**, 22 Kânchev St, tel: (0677) 22-47. **Veliko Târnovo Archaeological Museum**, for guides, tel: (062) 63-8841.

6
The Black Sea Coast

The attractive, sandy Bulgarian seacoast is one of the country's biggest assets and has been busy receiving visitors – wanted and unwanted – since antiquity. The first prehistoric peoples, who left behind the oldest gold treasure in the world near Varna, gave way to the Thracians, who competed and cohabited with Greek colonists in Varna, Nessebâr and Sozopol. The Romans stayed for five centuries, leaving the impressive Thermae in Varna and a smattering of walls and buildings. The Byzantines and medieval Bulgarians built dozens of basilicas in Nessebâr.

The two port towns and gateways to the distinctive southern and northern coasts are Burgas and Varna, respectively. The southern coast is warmer, quieter and lined with the last unspoilt beaches. The northern coast has all the major resorts like Golden Sands, Sunny Beach, Sveti Konstantin and Albena. Most coastal towns are vibrant and lively in the summer, and often quite crowded north of Sozopol. Outdoor restaurants and open-air festivals and fairs add to the festive mood.

The blend of ancient ruins, Revival architecture, quality museums and natural beauty makes the Black Sea coast a rewarding destination even for those that are allergic to crowded beaches. The Pobiti Kamâni rock formations near Varna, the green slopes of the remote Strandja Nature Park in the far south, the mellow Botanical Gardens at the Palace of Balchik – in these places you can be in the midst of nature by the sea but away from the beach crowds.

DON'T MISS

*** Sozopol and Nessebâr: cobbled streets, ancient remains and Revival houses.
*** Varna's Archaeological Museum: the world's oldest gold treasure, ancient necropolis.
** Maritime Garden in Burgas and Seaside Park in Varna: giant old trees and statues by the sea.
*** The Botanical Gardens at the Palace of Balchik: eclectic royal residence and eccentric gardens.
*** Beach life: swim, surf, lounge about with an ice cream.
*** Strandja Nature Park: hike for sea views in Bulgaria's largest park.

Opposite: *A crowded beach in Sozopol.*

CLIMATE

The southern coast is Mediterranean-influenced and has slightly higher temperatures. Summer (June to early September) has an average temperature of 24°C (73°F), though it can go over 30°C (86°F). The summer heat is tempered by breezes and nights are never hot. Autumn (September–October) is pleasant and warm, while spring and winter bring thunderstorms. Ice is common, and snow falls at least once between December and February on the northern coast.

KALIAKRA LEGENDS AND FACTS

At Cape Kaliakra's entrance, a Socialist-era stone sculpture depicting some proletarian-looking maidens immortalizes a local legend. When the inevitable Turks descended on the town, forty local girls tied their long tresses together and jumped off the cliff here, to avoid rape and enslavement. The cape also witnessed piracy of passing ships by the local population who lured them with coastal fires; many shipwrecks; and the final naval battle of the Russian-Turkish war in 1791. Every year, hippies and alternative life-stylers come to play guitars and make love not war at sunrise on 1 July.

Cape Kaliakra ★★

Bulgaria's easternmost cape plunges 70m (230ft) into the sea at Cape Kaliakra. The Kaliakra Nature Reserve (687ha/1698 acres), which includes the cape, is a peaceful area of rock caves (left by the Sarmatians in the 3rd–5th centuries), endemic plants, and 150 species of birds in the wetlands of Bolata and Taukliman north of the cape. The Kaliakra fortress was in turn Thracian, Roman, Bulgarian and Turkish, and has remains of churches, tombs and baths. Visit the Archaeological Museum, housed in a cave. Open 10:00–18:00. Spot dolphins in the early mornings or evenings.

Black Sea Coast

BALCHIK

Balchik is a picturesque, laid-back town of limestone cliffs and steep streets. The big attraction here is the Summer Palace and Botanical Gardens. Due to repeated natural and human destruction, you will spot only the occasional ruin of the Roman town Dionisopolis and the medieval town that stood here. Balchik didn't peak again until the 19th century when the wheat trade brought prosperity. There are only man-made beaches here, but if you want to be away from the crowds, Balchik offers authentic small-town atmosphere.

Summer Palace and Botanical Gardens ★★★

Follow the waterfront promenade 2.5 km (1.5 miles) west of the town and you'll reach the romantic Summer Palace of Queen Marie of Romania. The fertile plains of Dobrudja in northeast Bulgaria went to Romania after the Balkan Wars, and the eccentric, cultivated Queen Marie built her 'quiet nest' here. The 'Palace' itself, designed by Italian architects, is an eclectic Bulgarian Revival-style house with a minaret and a chapel among other things. The gorgeous Gardens house Mediterranean plants and 250 species of cacti, the second biggest cactus collection in Europe after Monaco. Among rumbling waterworks and ponds with giant lilies are scattered the sculptures and artefacts brought by the eclectic Queen Marie: Moorish archways stand next to Moroccan amphorae, a Hellenic marble throne, Muslim tombs, a Roman bath and Bessarabian monastery stone crosses. It comes as no surprise that the Queen was a follower of the tolerant Baha'ism philosophy and opened the Palace to Baha'i visitors. Open 09:00–18:00.

Albena, Golden Sands, Riviera and Sveti Konstantin

Of these four major purpose-built beach resorts recommended only to beach-bunnies, Sv Konstantin is the least built-up and quietest at night. The beaches are decent, but if water sports are your thing, head elsewhere. The mineral baths are the main attraction here; take a look also at the St Konstantin and St Elena Church which gave its name to the resort. Albena, less frantic than Golden Sands, is lively and boasts a beautiful 4km (2.4-mile) long beach and

Below: *Bulgaria has some wonderful beaches on the Black Sea Coast.*

great water sports. Golden Sands or Zlatni Pyasatsi lives
up to its name with a glorious 5km (3-mile) long beach, a
very noisy nightlife, and not much else. Riviera is set in a
lush park, and is made up of luxury hotels catering for the
local new rich.

Euxinograd Palace ★

Some 8km (5 miles) north of Varna is the former summer
residence for Prince Alexander of Battenberg, now a gov-
ernmental residence. Built in 1882 in a French château
style, it is worth visiting for its cellars and for the wine and
brandy which are bottled on the premises. Wander in the
lovely gardens and down a path to the secluded beach.

Aladja Monastery ★★

The monks who lived in this curious 40m (131ft) high rock-
hewn monastery from the 13th century until the 18th were
of the Hesychast order, like the hermits of the Ivanovo
Rock Monastery (see page 118). Climbing into the tiny,
bare cells hacked into the limestone cliffs, you'll be unsur-
prised to learn that Hesychasm was an ascetic Eastern
Orthodox teaching which required from the hermit solitude
and continuous prayer. As early as the 1st century AD,
Christians congregated here to perform their rituals, and
before them the Thracians performed theirs, leaving behind
megalithic monuments. Aladja means 'colourful' in Arabic
but sadly, erosion has done its work and the church murals
are gone, making the
austere whiteness of these
rock dwellings even more
ascetic. Some 600m (656yd)
down a path, you'll find the
Catacombs, another similar
rock dwelling. The one-
hour walk from Sveti
Konstantin passes through a
lovely forest. Open 09:00–
18:00, winter 09:00–16:00
and closed Monday and
Tuesday.

Below: *Inside a rock-hewn
cell, Aladja Monastery.*

VARNA

Bulgaria's Black Sea capital
and third city has a vibrant,
7000-year-old history of a
seaport at a crossroads. In
summer when the Seaside
Garden with its ancient
columns comes to life, you
can picture the merchants,
here at the bustling Greek
town of Odessos (founded
by the Miletian Greeks in
the 6th century BC), trading
wheat, wine, animal hides,
ceramics and jewellery. The
charm of modern Varna,
however, comes from its
handsome, recently restored
turn-of-the-century buildings in the spacious

pedestrianized area, the dolce vita atmosphere, the fine
museums, and the Varna Summer Festival. There is an
attractive urban beach adjacent to the Garden, and a constellation of bars and restaurants along the waterfront.

Varna Archaeological Museum ★★★

Set in a small garden off Mariya Luiza St, this is probably
Bulgaria's most interesting and complete museum, even
though it showcases only the Varna region. Among its
100,000 chronologically displayed exhibits is the most
impressive prehistoric necropolis in Europe with the world's
oldest crafted gold, circa 4600–4200BC; the chieftain of the
tribe was buried with 900 gold objects weighing 6kg (13lb).
You will also find clay figurines and pottery from the nearby
Neolithic settlement at Durankulak Lake, home to one of
the first European civilizations; Thracian tombs from 5BC;
statues from the Hellenic period (there was a temple of
Apollo in Odessos); impressive Roman mosaics and necropoli from the 1st–3rd centuries AD; exquisite Byzantine
jewellery from the 5th–6th centuries; a large collection of

Above: *Varna Cathedral.*

16th–18th-century icons. The outdoor café in the lovely courtyard is a haven from the modernity of the outside world. Open 10:00–17:00, closed on Mon; in winter closed on Mon and Sun.

Varna Art Gallery ★★

This handsomely presented gallery offers an overview of 20th-century Bulgarian fine art and sculpture, plus some 17th-century West European art. Open 10:00–17:00, closed Monday.

Roman Thermae ★★★

These impressive public baths (circa 2nd century) are the largest ancient building in Bulgaria. Built during the revival of Odessos by the Romans over 7.2km² (2.8 sq miles), surprisingly large chunks of it stand despite the poor maintenance. The hypocaust (underground heating system) and underground sewage pipes are particularly interesting. Look for the marked halls – *apodyterium* (changing rooms), *frigidarium* (cold water room), *tepidarium* (tepid water room), *caldarium* (hot water pool), and the 60m (66yd) long open-air *palaestra* (social space) where the bathers gathered to play sports, gossip and listen to poets and orators. The good times ended with the decline of the Western Roman Empire and, two centuries later, stones and statues were lifted from here to build the nearby 6th-century Odessos Baths (only worth seeing in passing). Curiously, medieval craftsmen held their workshops here in the 14th century. Open 10:00–17:00, closed Monday, in winter closed Mon and Sun.

The Cathedral of the Assumption of the Virgin ★★

It is the massive size of this modern-looking, late 19th-century cathedral rather than its artistic worth that makes it

---

IS THE BLACK SEA BLACK?

Of course not. The Bulgarian belief is that the name Black comes from the severe winter storms in this small landlocked sea, i.e. it's dark and dangerous. The ancient Greeks called it 'Inhospitable' (presumably to invaders), then, after much of it was colonized by them, they renamed it 'Hospitable'. Many natural and induced shipwrecks occurred along the shores, especially near capes like Shabla, Kaliakra, Emine and Maslen Nos – which means Oily Cape, named after the many Greek olive-oil carrying ships that shattered here. Somehow, all this has produced the 'Black' Sea.

remarkable. One of the three altars is dedicated to 13th-century Russian ruler and prince, Alexander Nevski. The canny priests will charge you for taking photographs. Open 07:00–22:00.

The Seaside Garden ★★

It stretches 8km (5 miles) along the waterfront, and houses several attractions suitable for children: the Dolphinarium (if you can be at Cape Kaliakra early in the morning or at sunset, you're better off seeing dolphins in the wild); the Aquarium (bul. Primorski 4, 08:00–19:00, winter 10:00–16:00 and closed weekends); and the Summer Theatre where concerts and shows in the Varna Summer Festival (June–August) are often held.

AROUND VARNA
Pobiti Kamâni (Stone Forest) ★★★

A bizarre stone forest grows in a sandy steppe 18km (11 miles) west of Varna on the old road to Sofia. These porous limestone columns reach 9m (29.5ft) in height and assume curious shapes and patterns reminiscent of mystic rituals. Indeed, even if their geological origin is generally dated to 50 million years ago when southeast Europe was the bottom of a sea, their actual formation and symbolism is the subject of speculation. There are several groups of these stony trees; the

> ## DOBRICH
>
> For a glimpse at the fertile plains of Dobrudja, the north-east corner of Bulgaria, take a day trip to the pleasant inland town of Dobrich, 54km (33.5 miles) from Varna. The small but perfectly formed Dobrich Ethnographic Complex has authentic 19th-century workshops and shops, and a modest but interesting Archaeological Museum (08:00–17:00, closed weekends) where you can see swords from the Crusader army of Vladislav Varnenchik, jewellery from the nomadic tribes who passed through here, a reconstructed necropolis from 4000BC, and a curious collection of medieval mace tips.

Below: Pobiti Kamâni Stone Forest.

SUNNY BEACH

This is Golden Sands' ever-popular terrible twin: massive 8km (5-mile) long beach, three- and four-star hotels, and noisy families. The setting among parklands makes it reasonably pleasant, however. Just north of it across the bay from Nessebâr is the soulless, built-up new resort Sveti Vlas whose pretty views of Nessebâr are its only redeeming feature.

most accessible is the Dikilitash group by the road. Look out for harmless lizards and snakes (and harmful vipers).

Kamchiya Reserve ★★

Take a boat ride 30km (18.6 miles) south of Varna along the estuary of the Kamchiya River in the Longoza biosphere – one of the quietest and loveliest corners of the northern coast. This wet grove is a lush tangle of protected endemic trees and ivies, populated with birds, reptiles and water turtles. North of the estuary is a shallow, fine-sand beach.

NESSEBÂR

The cultural highlight of the seacoast, UNESCO-protected Nessebâr is an atmospheric, open-air museum to medieval Eastern art. For many centuries it was a bustling, privileged trading port. The town walls you pass through to enter the peninsula from the long, thin isthmus that links it to the mainland were the original work of the Thracians. The Dorian Greeks who arrived in the 6th century fortified the town, called it Messambria and proceeded to prosper from its ports. Messambrians wisely surrendered without resistance to the Romans in 72BC, unlike their southern rival Sozopol/Apolonia. Later, it frequently changed hands between the Byzantines and the Bulgarians, and managed to avoid complete devastation even when it fell to the Turks.

Below: *Nessebâr.*

Although the beautiful wooden 19th-century houses make it a great place for strolling, the attraction here is the exquisite medieval Byzantine-Bulgarian churches in the form of ruins, museums and art galleries. The old town is less than a kilometre long and easy to see in a few hours – which is what the busloads of tourists do. To avoid the crush, arrive early in the morning or late in the afternoon, or tour the island along the quiet waterside promenade. The new town

across the isthmus is of little interest except for its hotels, restaurants and market.

Archaeological Museum ★

This small but well-formed (though not always well-labelled) museum contains some compelling objects that take you through the many lives of Messambria/ Nessebâr, starting with gold jewellery and tomb tablets from a 4th-century BC necropolis. Later highlights are the medieval ceramics and the giant gilded icon of the Virgin with Jesus made in 1342 for Tsar Ivan Alexander who took Nessebâr from Byzantium. Call (0554) 46-012 to book an English guide. Open 09:00–18:00, winter 09:00–12:00, 12:30–17:00, weekends 09:00–17:00.

Tour of Nessebâr's Churches ★★★

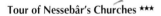

We start at the green space along Metropolitska Street, and continue clockwise around the island. Note the characteristic Byzantine style of layered white stone and red brick, and blind niches.

Pantokrator

A paragon of medieval Eastern Orthodox architecture, the 13th–14th-century Hristos Pantocrator Church stands out with its coloured ceramic decoration and round bell tower. It is open as an art gallery, 09:00–23:00, winter 10:00–17:00.

St John the Baptist (Sveti Yoan Krastitel)

This attractive, pink-hued 10th–11th century church is well preserved and marks the transition from shortened basilica to cruciform domed church. The art gallery inside contains some fabulous artworks, and beautifully restored frescoes from the 13th and 17th centuries, including one of Saint Marina. The Ottomans turned the building into stables for a time. Open 10:00–20:00, winter 10:00–16:00.

Above: *Pantokrator has a round bell tower.*

Above: *The ruins of the 9th-century Basilica.*

St Spas (Sveti Spas)

Unremarkable from the outside thanks to the Ottoman law of Christian buildings not surpassing a metre above ground, this 1609 church has interesting and well-preserved frescoes from the 17th-century Nessebâr art school. There are two curious things: the Islamic flower motifs painted by the artists to placate the Turks, and the rare (in Bulgaria) image of Christ ascending in a 'capsule' of light. Open 10:00–17:30.

Nessebâr Orthodox Church

Visit if you would like to attend a service at a modern Bulgarian church – this is the only functioning one in town.

Basilica St Sofia or Old Bishopric

Back onto ulitsa Mitropolitska (Bishop's St) are the central ruins of Nessebâr dating back to the 6th and 9th centuries – the former Bishopric. In 1257, the Venetians reduced this once glorious three-nave basilica to what you see now.

St Stefan

Closed for restoration until the end of 2008. This 11th-century church became the 'new Bishopric' after the misfortune of the Basilica. It has well-preserved frescoes, the medieval bishop's throne, and a 16th-century iconostasis.

St John Aliturgetos

Perched above the harbour is Nessebâr's most elaborate former church, partially destroyed by an earthquake. Built in the 14th century with mixed masonry, it has, unusually, two entrances. This is a lovely spot to watch the boats moored in the harbour below, then follow the remains of Messambria's city walls down to the seaside promenade.

BURGAS

Burgas is Bulgaria's major port and coastal gateway. It shares with Varna its history of Greek settlers, a glorious Maritime Park, and laid-back, pedestrian summer streets shaded by leafy trees. Although its charm is less glamorous, its turn-of-the-century buildings less attractive than those of Varna, and its urban beach does not come recommended, Burgas is a pleasant, compact town and an ideal base from which to explore Sozopol and Nessebâr. The main shopping and people-watching streets are Aleksandrovska and Aleko Bogoridi. Burgas is surrounded by four easy-to-reach lakes rich in flora and home to a staggering 60% of Bulgaria's bird life.

Maritime Park ★★★

This gorgeous waterside park lines the east side of Burgas and is peaceful in the daytime and lively at night. Among the ivy-covered trees, well-kept flower beds and fountains are scattered monuments and statues, including a small monument of gratitude from the Armenians of Burgas to

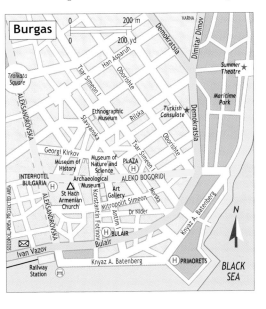

LAGOONS

A few kilometres south of Sozopol are the lush lagoons of Alepu and Arkutino, an ideal getaway when the crowds of Sozopol get too much. Alepu has an attractive wild beach, but Arkutino is the more interesting one, with dense semi-tropical vegetation and 40m (131ft) high sand-dunes. Access by private transport.

DEULTUM-DEBELT

Some 20km (12.4 miles) south of Burgas on the 79 road, the Roman Emperor Vespasian (69–79AD) gave land to the veterans of the 8th legion, and here they built a fortified town they called Deultum. From the 8th century onwards, this became the fortified rampart of Debelt, a disputed borderland between the Byzantine empire and the Bulgarian kingdom whose armies regularly made gruesome depredations on each other's civilians. Some of the excavated Roman, Byzantine and Bulgarian remains are in the Burgas Archaelogical Museum, but most are in the local Debelt Museum by the side of the road to Burgas. Like Nikopolis-ad-Istrum and many other ancient sites in Bulgaria, Debelt is threatened by lack of funding and protection. Visit only in an organized tour.

their Bulgarian compatriots, and a bas-relief of the Polish writer Adam Mickiewicz who lived here in 1850. The Summer Theatre houses the colourful International Folkloric Festival in August.

Archaeological Museum ★
A humble cousin to the Sozopol Museum and better than its Nessebâr counterpart, it has some fascinating regional finds from Thracian, Roman and Greek times. Among the most curious and unusual exhibits are the oldest statue in Bulgaria, circa 5th century BC, the amazing gold jewellery of a Thracian woman from the 1st century BC, a wooden coffin of a the 2nd-century Roman soldier, and 'arrow-coins' from the 6th century BC which predated the use of coins. One room is dedicated to Develt, the Roman colony nearby (see panel). Located halfway down the pedestrian Aleko Bogoridi St, it is open 08:00–12:00 and 13:00–18:00 (winter 13:00–17:00), closed Sunday.

St Hach Armenian Church ★
This modest little church next to the immodest Hotel Bulgaria was built in the mid-19th century by the local Armenian community with Bulgarian help. Its interior is touching in its homeliness. In the courtyard is a memorial to the Armenian genocide of 1915. Open 08:30–17:00.

Museums ★
A far cry from Varna's museums are the Art Gallery housed in a 1909 synagogue; the History Museum which is planning a new section on ethnic minorities and city history; and the Ethnographic Museum which has interesting regional costumes and temporary exhibitions.

The Burgas Lakes ★★
Surrounding Burgas in a remarkable juxtaposition of industrial port city and unspoilt biosphere, these four lakes – Pomorie, Atanasovsko, Mandra and Burgasko – make up Bulgaria's largest wetland reserve and contain a dense array of protected birds and mammals. The Pomorie Lake is the furthest to the north, and the largest is Burgas Lake,

rich in pelicans and cormorants. The easiest place to visit, just south of Burgas on the road to Sozopol, is the Poda Protected Area: take the enchanting nature trail to see nesting and migratory birds. Alternatively, contact the Poda Centre to arrange a visit (see At a Glance, page 111).

SOZOPOL

The most charming town on the seacoast has been Nessebâr's rival since the Dorian Greeks founded Messambria and the Miletian Greeks settled in Apollonia in the 7th–6th centuries BC. Named after the Greek god of the sun and the arts, Apollonia did brisk trade with Athens and Rhodes in olives, wine, jewellery, pottery, honey and textiles. When the Romans took the town by force in the 1st century AD, they sent the symbol of the polis – a 13m (43ft) high bronze statue of Apollo – to Rome. What remains of those prosperous and eventful times is the rampart wall running along the old town's waterfront, with restaurants perched on top; the rest is in the renovated Archaeological Museum. Unlike Nessebâr, old Sozopol's attraction lies in the atmospheric stone-and-wood Revival houses and cobbled lanes, the street artists and old women selling lace and jams, and the mellow harbour whose fishing boats are named after women. Although the bohemian spirit of the town has been tarred in recent years by rampant commercialization, the old town is much less tacky and more lived-in than Nessebâr. There are several good beaches, and the new town, built in the early 20th century, has most of the accommodation.

Archaeological Museum **

Predictably, the focus here is on life in Apollonia. You can see the country's largest collection of antique painted ceramics and plastic art, a bevy of stone anchors circa

Below: *Fishing boats bobbing in the harbour at Sozopol.*

Right: *Sozopol.*

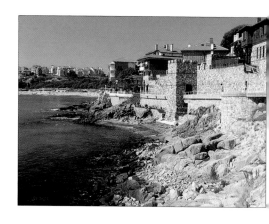

4000BC, and fascinating replicas of the ships in which different civilizations sailed into Apollonia's harbour over the centuries – Phoenicians, Cypriots, Romans and Egyptians. Located at Khan Krum Square; go down the steps. Open 08:00–17:00 every day, winter 08:00–12:00, closed Sunday and Monday.

Art Gallery ★★

Sitting atop a scenic bluff at the northeast tip of the peninsula, this beautiful house contains sea-themed art by renowned local painters. Open 08:30–18:30.

St Zossim Chapel ★

Sozopol, a name adopted by the town in the 4th century, means 'town of salvation', i.e. for the saved mariners and sailors. The bodies of those who died, however, were displayed in this 9th–13th-century chapel named after the patron saint of sailors, in the little seaside park at the top of the Town Beach.

Sveta Bogoroditsa (Church of the Virgin Mary) ★★

Built in the 17th century, partially underground on top of a medieval church, it contains an exquisite iconostasis and a Bishop's throne carved by artists from Macedonia's Debâr school. Located at Anaksimander St, opening times vary – best to ask at the Archaeological Museum.

Beaches

The sheltered Town Beach has adequate (shallow) water and amenities. The much larger and more exposed Harmanite in the new town is lined with bars and fruit stalls, and the far end is for nudists.

Ropotamo Nature Reserve ★★

Further south is the shady Ropotamo estuary, where you can go on a boat cruise down the river and see birds, reptiles and water lilies, or take short hikes in the primeval forest.

STRANDJA NATURE PARK ★★★

The exotic corner of southeastern Bulgaria, in contrast with the swarming seaside, is a well-kept secret. The low-lying Mediterranean ranges of Strandja spread over the Bulgarian-Turkish border and reach only 700m (2297ft) in Bulgaria. This fertile stretch of 1161km^2 (721 sq miles) is home to a staggering 50% of the country's vegetation and 70% of the bird life. Among the soft green hills of Strandja and the stunning gorges of the Veleka River are scattered the barely excavated remains of many civilizations: caves marked by prehistoric people, stone sundials, Thracian tombs, Greek columns, Roman road fragments, medieval fortresses and stone carvings in shady forests. Some of the findings can be seen in the Malko Târnovo town museum, tel: (05952) 29-98. Sleepy Malko (Little) Târnovo is the only town among underpopulated and eerie villages like Bulgari (see panel) and Brâshlyan.

Tourism in Strandja lags behind due to its proximity with the border, and it doesn't have the infrastructure for mass tourism, which is part of its charm. Accommodation is scarce in this camper's paradise, but the hiking possibilities are plentiful: Bulgari-Silkossia Reserve-Kosti village on the Veleka River (14km/8.6 miles) for easy forest paths and scenic views; Malko Târnovo-Daskalite-dolmen tomb in Propada area (8km/5 miles) for rare plants, birds and ruins; Malko Târnovo-Manastircheto area-Mogilata area-Buchvarka fountain (8km/5 miles) for great views; Sinemorets-against the Veleka stream-Brodilovo village (20km/12.4 miles) for riverside wildlife and transition from sea to mountain.

The Black Sea Coast at a Glance

Late June to early September is the beach season. The heat is rarely oppressive thanks to the sea breezes (average 23°C/ 73.4°F), and nights are pleasantly cool. To escape crowds but avoid snow, the cool early summer (May–June) and the mild autumn (mid- to late Sept, early Oct) are the best times. Most hotels close in winter.

The E773 Sofia-Burgas and E772 Sofia-Varna roads are in good condition. Several daily buses and flights go from Sofia to the coast. Several daily buses leave Burgas for Bulgari/Malko Târnovo in Strandja, but best access is by car. The road from Tsarevo on the coast to Malko Târnovo is in poor shape.

Regular buses go between all towns, convenient for day-trips. If you visit places like Kaliakra, Strandja, Pobiti Kamâni and Aladja Monastery, it is best to arrange your own transport. Mini-buses go between Burgas and Slânchev Bryag every half hour, and several daily buses to Sozopol and Nessebâr.

The Northeast
Villa Kibela, tel: (02) 87-18878, www.villakibela.com North of Kaliakra Cape near Durankulak Lake in an unspoilt coastal area near Romanian border. The English-speaking hosts can organize activities like fishing,

biking, caving, bird-watching, etc. Sleeps and feeds 15 people in tasteful luxury.
Albena, Golden Sands, Sveti Konstantin, Riviera and Sunny Beach. These resorts consist of hotels only and we cannot give specific recommendations. Prices are high, all hotels are either refurbished or new, and the standard of accommodation and food is generally high.

Varna
BUDGET/MID-RANGE
Hotel Cherno More (Black Sea), 33 Slivnitsa Bvld, tel: (052) 61-2235, www.chernomorebg.com The best deal in town, this renovated three-star hotel has top location, budget prices and great views.
Villa Sagona, Sea Garden, tel: (052) 30-3783, villasagona@mail.bg A 1930s villa with huge rooms, idyllic by day and great for park walks, but hard to find at night. Fine restaurant.
Hotel Odessos, 1 Slivnitsa St, (052) 64-0300, www.odessos-bg.com At Gardens entrance, noisy but friendly and comfortable. Get a room with a view.

LUXURY
Grand Hotel Musala Palace, 3 Musala St, tel: (052) 66-4175, www.musalapalace.bg Sumptuous *belle-époque* five-star boutique hotel in a 100-year-old landmark building in the heart of Varna. Spa, gourmet restaurant, gym.
Art Hotel, 59 Preslav St, tel: (052) 65-7600, www.hotels-bg.com/arthotel Exquisite retro

boutique hotel near Musala Palace. Great value, stylish bar.

Nessebâr
Hotels pack out in July–August, so book early.

MID-RANGE
Hotel Prince Cyril, 9 Slavyanska, tel: (0554) 42-215, princecyril_hotel@abv.bg Comfortable family hotel in the heart of the old town. Restaurant Prince Cyril is next door.

LUXURY
Iberostar Festa Panorama, new town, tel: (0554) 29-700. Four-star with sea views, walking distance from old town.
Hotel Monte Cristo, 2 Venera St, old town. Boutique hotel between two ancient churches.

Burgas
LUXURY
Interhotel Bulgaria, 21 Alexandrovska St, tel: (056) 84-1501, www.bulgaria-hotel.com The ugly building belies the comfortable, refurbished rooms and four-star facilities.

MID-RANGE
Plaza Hotel, 42 Bogoridi St, tel: (056) 84-6294, www.plazahotel-bg.com Stylish business hotel. Free Internet. The huge suite with two bathrooms is recommended.
Hotel Primorets, 2 Knyaz Batemberg St, south end of Maritime Park, tel: (056) 84-1417, www.hotelprimoretz.com Comfortable rooms and sea views from the balconies.

The Black Sea Coast at a Glance

Hotel Bulair, 7 Bulair St, tel: (056) 84-4389. New hotel, conveniently located between the Park and Alexandrovska St.

Sozopol
LUXURY/MID-RANGE
Hotel Villa List, 5 Cherno More St, tel/fax: (0550) 22-235, www.hotellist-bg.com Good location in new town, lovely light-filled rooms with views.
Hotel Parnasse, 3 Lazuren Bryag St, tel: (0550) 24-412, www.parnasse-bg.com Overlooking the old town, comfortable bright rooms. Sauna.

BUDGET
Hotel Boruna, 51 Odessa St, tel/fax: (0550) 22-872, www.boruna.holiday.bg Three-star family hotel in the new town.
Rusalka, 36 Millet St, tel: (0550) 23-047, doneva_sp@abv.bg On sea-promenade in old town, breakfast included.

Strandja
Private homes in villages like Brâshlyan are the cosiest option. Otherwise:
Hotel Hipocrat, Malko Târnovo, tel: (05952) 28-14. Basic.
Sarmashik, Brâshlyan, tel: (05952) 28-44. Comfortable.

Balchik
There are bar-grill and fish restaurants west of the town port.

Sveti Konstantin
Sirius Boat-Restaurant, tel: (052) 36-1932. Fabulous fish restaurant in a boat on a cliff.

Dâlboka Mussel Farm and Restaurant, on the road from Kaliakra and Kavarna, turn off at Bulgarevo. Delicious seafood right on the water. Note: the turn-off to the coast is steep.

Varna
Enotekata, 20 Koloni St, tel: (052) 60-5061. Stylish wine-bar and restaurant, international food. Near E. Yossif Place.
Bulgaverna Nashenci, 27A Tsar Simeon St, tel: (052) 63-0186. Themed, balconied Bulgarian restaurant, live music. Get the table in the shape of a well.
Prodadena Nevesta, 1 Krali Marko St (near the Opera), tel: 088-8641440. Stylish tavern serving European food, huge wine and spirit selection.
Bistro Evropa, 11 Slivnitsa Blvd, tel: (052) 60-3950. Fresh clams, fabulous pastries/cakes.
Orient, 1 Tsaribrod St, tel: (052) 60-2380. Excellent Turkish and Middle Eastern food. Narghile lounge upstairs.

Nessebâr
Kapitanska Sreshta, 2 Mena St, tel: (0554) 42-124. Fine Mediterranean *mehana* in a period house overlooking the harbour.
Bistro Aquamarin, 3 Kraibrejna St, tel: (00554) 42-091. Fish fare in folk décor, lovely views.
Lozarska Kashta, 4 Khan Asparuh, tel: (0554) 43-164. Traditional food, warm indoors, pleasant courtyard.

Burgas
Bohem, 46 Alexandrovska St, tel: (056) 82-6091. Pseudo-retro décor, decent bistro food.
Burgaska Sreshta, Knyaz Batemberg, opposite Hotel Primoretz, (056) 43-161. Fine up-market dining in period house with lovely garden.
Hemingway, 8 Rilska St, tel: (056) 82-1208. Classy seafood.

Sozopol
Ksantana, 7 Morski Skali, tel: (0550) 22-454. Great fish, great sea views, a favourite.
Vyatârna Melnitsa (The Windmill), 27 Morski Skali, tel: (0550) 22-844. Folk-themed restaurant serving Bulgarian food and wines; live music. Also try **Stenata**, **Sozopol Tavern**, or **Neptune**.

Branta Tours, tel: (05743) 2259, www.branta-tours.com Birdwatching and wildlife tours along the coast. In Burgas, **Vera Tours** organizes visits to nearby sites, tel: (056) 27-577.

Varna Tourist Information Centre, Mussala Place, at the heart of the pedestrian zone.
Etap and Bio Met Tourist Agencies, next to Hotel Cherno More, organize tours, transport, car rentals. **The Tourist Bureau** in Hotel Bulgaria in Burgas offers help with tours and transport. **Poda Nature Centre**, tel: (056) 56 85-0540. **Strandja National Park office**, 1 Yanko Maslinkov St, Malko Târnovo, tel: (05952) 28-96.
Strandja travel services and information, heal@dir.bg

7
The Danube

Danubian Bulgaria, once prosperous and busy, is now the least visited part of the country – both by locals and foreigners. This is largely due to the depressed economy in the north and the bad roads (which are apparently getting fixed). Many factories closed along the Danube with the fall of Communism, and very high unemployment has resulted in mass emigration to Sofia and abroad. With the exception of Ruse, one of the loveliest cities of Bulgaria, none of the places profiled here are prosperous or happy, but they are well worth visiting for their natural beauty, historic richness and unaffected people – and for an interesting glimpse into some of the least touristy corners of Bulgaria.

It is possible to drive along the Danube, but it is not a particularly scenic river, and the places to visit are to the west and east, with nothing of real interest in between. It is therefore best to explore the sights in this section in two separate trips: Belogradchik and Vidin from Sofia or the Balkan Ranges, and Ruse, Rusenski Lom Park and Silistra from the Balkan Ranges or from the seacoast. The tourist infrastructure in these places has improved massively in the last few years thanks to the Beautiful Bulgaria Project and entrepreneurial individuals: new family hotels have sprung up, brochures printed, historic buildings restored, and museums fight to stay open. There are only two scenic spots from which to enjoy the Danube, however – the Silistra and Vidin waterside parks.

DON'T MISS

★★★ **Belogradchik Rocks and Fort:** spectacular rock formations stretching for 30km (19 miles), and a scenic fort.
★★★ **The Baba Vida Fortress in Vidin:** a fully preserved medieval fortress on the Danube.
★★★ **Loitering in Ruse:** Bulgaria's most European-looking city.
★★★ **The Ivanovo Rock Monastery:** medieval rock-hewn dwellings near Ruse.
★★ **Medjidi Tabia Fortress in Silistra:** Turkish fortress with interesting history.

Vrachanska Balkan and Iskâr Gorge ★★

If you take the slow, scenic road or railway from Sofia to Mezdra on your way north, you will travel along the spec-

Opposite: *The streets of Ruse are lined with beautiful period buildings.*

Below: *Belogradchik Fortress.*

tacular Iskâr Gorge. It cuts through the Balkan Ranges, and the huge cliffs you see belong to the little-visited Vrachanska Balkan National Park. Stop to see the whitewashed Cherepish Monastery, go for a short hike from the main square in small, dramatically set Vratsa 29km (18 miles) up the road, and visit Ledenika Cave 15km (9.5 miles) from Vratsa. The enchanting new Vrachanska eco-trail outside Vratsa takes you across small bridges and rumbling forests.

BELOGRADCHIK

This friendly, picturesque 'Small White Town' huddled at the western end of the Balkan Ranges has one of Bulgaria's most stunning natural phenomena, overseen by one of the most panoramic fortresses. Mass tourism hasn't arrived yet, but it's a popular base for rock-climbing and visiting prehistoric caves nearby, like the Magura Cave.

The Belogradchik Rocks ★★★

Spreading for 30 surreal km (20 miles) around Belogradchik, the simply named Rocks are far from simple. Some 200 million years ago this was the bottom of an ocean, which emerged with the formation of the Balkan Ranges as a fantastical landscape of reddish sedimentary rocks. The central group starts right in the middle of town. Go down the steps from the main square and wander among the petrified forest's many trails. Sunset and early morning are particularly inspiring, but don't hang out in the 'forest' at night.

The Fortress (Kaleto) ★★★

Walk the 2km (1.2 miles) from town to the breath-taking fortress winding up a huge outcrop of rocks. The Romans built it in the 1st–3rd centuries as an observation post over the strategic Danube road. The Byzantines and medieval Bulgarians improved it, and finally the Turks made it impregnable and used it to

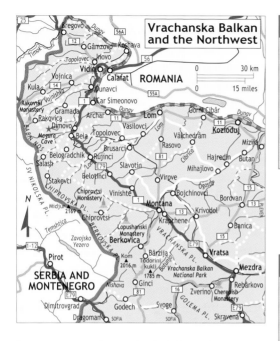

CLIMATE

The Danubian Plain can have a harsh climate due to central European influences. Ruse and Silistra have the highest summer temperatures in the country (35°C/95°F), and winters are snowy. Late spring to early summer (May–June) and early autumn (September) are the best times to visit.

house a garrison and put out local rebellions. The most infamous of those was the unsuccessful 1850 uprising in the northwest, drowned in blood as Bulgarian prisoners were beheaded inside the fortress. It's a glorious place to clamber around and take in the sweeping views over the town and the Rocks. Open 09:00–18:00, winter 09:00–17:00.

Magura Cave ★★★

The Belogradchik area is rich in caves, the best known and studied of which is 17km (10.5 miles) northwest of Belogradchik. The Magura is one of the largest caves in the country, 2500m (8202ft) long, and one of the oldest – 15 million years old. This has produced not only stupendous halls and massive stalagmites and stalactites, but also several hundred prehistoric drawings, including a solar calendar in the Sanctuary Hall. These fascinating naïve images of animals, hunters, plants and male and female figures date from 10,000BC onwards. Inside the cave you can taste and buy

CAVING

The Belogradchik area is paradise for extreme sports fans. Apart from the Rocks, which are not entirely safe due to their crumbly nature, but nevertheless attract many climbers, the area abounds in all manner of exciting caves. Most of these should only be visited and explored by fit people, and with a trained guide (see panel, page 120). They fall into three groups: dry, water, and precipice caves. A few are only recently discovered and not fully explored, such as the Martin-11 precipice cave, 92m (301ft) deep. For the average punter the Magura Cave is exciting enough, but if you need extra thrills, the Desni Sukhi Pech dry cave near Dolni Lom and the Venets dry cave near Oreshets are accessible without equipment (access to entrance only by car).

Above: *The 17th-century Stambul Kapiya wall-gate in Vidin.*

Magura champagne, and there's a restaurant next door. For visits, call (0936) 3161.

VIDIN

Vidin, the westernmost town in Danubian Bulgaria, is a pleasant backwater with an attractive waterside park and a formidable riverside fortress. The town's sleepy present stands in contrast with its glorious past, about which you can learn by walking alongside the park panels narrating the town's history. Bdin/Vidin was a medieval Tsars' stronghold, and later the most important commercial Ottoman port on the Danube. In the 18th century, the breakaway Turkish pasha Osman Pazvantoglu seceded Vidin from the Sultan's administration and this prosperous area became autonomous.

From the main square Bdintsi, where the 17th-century Ottoman wall-gate Stambul Kapiya faces the ex-Communist Party HQ, make your way to Baba Vida Fortress. You will pass the Krâstata Kazarma (Cross-shaped barracks), left by Osman Pazvantoglu, once used by Janissaries, then as a school, prison, hospital and tenement building, and now as an Ethnographic Museum. Stop also at the abandoned, eerily grand 19th-century Synagogue in Baba Vida Street.

BABA VIDA

Baba Vida means 'grandmother Vida', a curious name for a defence outpost used by a multinational succession of bloody-minded men. Legend goes that in the early Middle Ages, a powerful *boyar* (nobleman) had three daughters. Kula and Gâmza married badly and their husbands squandered their inherited fortunes. Vida didn't marry, but dedicated herself to serving her people and defending her lands from the fort she built, later named after her, presumably after she lived to an old age. Kula and Gâmzigrad, founded by Vida's prodigal sisters, are now small towns in Bulgaria and Serbia and Montenegro.

Baba Vida Fortress ★★★

Deceptively compact from the outside, this ancient moated fortress contains passageways, courtyards and towers. It is entirely preserved, unusual in a country where invasions have destroyed so much. The medieval Bulgarians built it on the foundations of the Roman fort Bononia. Despot Sishman attacked Serbia from here, which brought ruin on Bdin, but the town thrived later in the 14th century under Despot Ivan Stracimir. He built the 16m (52ft) Stracimir's tower, climbed up a hazardous ladder seemingly not repaired since then. Equally interesting are the workshops and living premises, the gallows where Bulgarian rebels were hanged by the Turks, the 10th-century tower next to it, and the tunnel for transporting cannons to the shooting terrace. Open 08:30–17:00, 10:00–17:00 weekends, winter 08:00–16:30.

RUSE

Ruse, the country's fifth largest city and the most European by its architecture and history, plays second fiddle today, but it was centre stage in the 19th century when many urban inventions were pioneered here – cinema, the first newspaper and the first railway in the Ottoman empire (to Varna). The Bridge of Friendship in Ruse is the river link with Romania. After the environmental crisis of the 1980s (*see* panel, page 119) and mass immigration of the 1990s, this 'little Vienna' is finally going through the revival it deserves. Although it lacks a riverside park, its beautiful period buildings, glorious main square, Svoboda (Freedom) Square, and laid-back pedestrian mall make it a pleasant place to spend a day or two. The Ivanovo Rock Monastery and medieval Cherven Fortress in the picturesque Rusenski Lom Park make a convenient day trip.

Sexaginta Prista ★

This Roman fort near the waterfront is where Ruse began under the Emperor Vespasian (AD69–79). It was connected to both Nikopolis-ad-Istrum (*see* Central Bulgaria) and Odesos (Varna). Not much of the 'Port of the 60 Ships' remains thanks to the depredations of Barbarian tribes in the 6th century, but the site offers a sweeping view over the Danube and some rather interesting Roman remains, tombs and pottery. Poorly signposted, look for the flight of stairs at the bottom of Kaloyan St. The fort is open 09:00–12:00, 13:00–17:00, closed weekends.

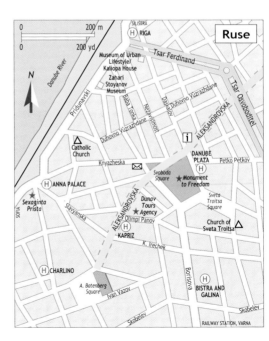

SHOPPING IN THE DANUBE AREA

There is good shopping in Ruse: **Craft Mall** for quality souvenirs, 20 Alexandrovska St; and **Artstyle Boutique**, 1 Raiko Daskalov St (closed Sun) for beautiful Bulgarian and international gifts.

St Troitsa Church ★★

The atmospheric early 17th-century Holy Trinity Church, the oldest surviving building in Ruse, descends dramatically underground via a wide staircase to comply with the Ottoman law about Christian buildings not exceeding one metre in height. The unusual stained-glass windows create a twilight atmosphere. It retains its original icons and murals (look out for the Cyril and Methodius fresco), and the grounds around it contain a medieval Christian cemetery. Open 07:00–19:00.

Museum of Urban Lifestyle/Kaliopa House ★★

The museum has a sumptuous display of urban lifestyle in 19th-century Bulgaria with exhibits from Ruse families. The house was previously occupied by the Turkish Consulate, and some say it was gifted by the local Turkish governor to his paramour Kaliopa, wife of the Prussian consul. Across from Riga Hotel. Open 09:00–12:00, 13:00–17:30, closed Sunday; for Saturday visits, call (082) 82-5002.

Below: *Rusenski Lom National Park.*

Rusenski Lom National Park

The beautifully varied Rusenski Lom Park south of Ruse comprises 3260ha (8055 acres) along the canyon of the Rusenski Lom River (which changes its name downstream several times). It is a paradise for hiking, bird-watching and caving. Among the rugged cliffs and hilltops nestle two scenic medieval places of interest.

Ivanovo Rock Monastery ★★★

About 20km (12.5 miles) south of Ruse, dizzyingly perched in a riverside cliff, the Ivanovo Rock Monastery is a fascinating memento of medieval hermit living. The 106 karst rock cells and 41 rock churches were inhabited by monks of the Hesychast order from the 14th to the 16th century when erosion drove them away. The church (currently open to visitors), Church of the Holy Virgin, contains remarkable murals considered to herald the European Renaissance and similar in their humanist, non-dogmatic style to the frescos in Boyana Church (see page 40). Note *The Last Supper*, painted 164 years before da Vinci's version, and again, as in Boyana, the portrait of the monastery *ktitors* (donors), the Bulgarian Tsar Ivan Alexander and his wife Theodora offering a rock representing the monastery to the Holy Virgin. Open 09:00–18:00 Tue–Sat, autumn/winter by arrangement, tel: (08116) 22-19 or (082) 82-5002.

Cherven Fortress ★★
Another 15km (9.5 miles) further south, the well-preserved hilltop fortress of Cherven dates back to the 6th century when Ruse dwellers fled here from Barbarian invasions. Cherven peaked as a major commercial and administrative town during the Second Bulgarian Kingdom. The remains of 11 churches, the citadel, streets, and the tunnel water system are better preserved than those in Tsarevets, and the restoration of Baldwin's Tower in Tsarevets was modelled on the defence tower here. Open Tue–Sat 09:00–13:00 and 14:00–18:00, winter by request, tel: (082) 82-5002.

Srebârna Nature Reserve ★
About 20km (12.5 miles) west of Silistra on the road to Ruse, the UNESCO-protected freshwater Srebârna Lake is home to 180 species of nesting and migratory birds. Walks and bird-watching visits can be arranged through the Museum of Natural History in Srebârna.

SILISTRA
Silistra is an economically depressed but pleasant town with a rich Roman history, a remarkable Turkish fortress, and a lovely riverside park with substantial Roman and Byzantine remains.

DANUBE DISASTERS

Relations between Bulgaria and Romania were strained in the 1980s due to a toxic chlorine and sodium leak in Romania which polluted the air of Bulgarian river cities for years. More recently, the 1999 NATO bombings of three Danubian bridges in Serbia and Montenegro made navigation difficult until 2002. Another massive industrial disaster in Romania in 2000 resulted in cyanide spills which killed much of the river's local wildlife, and was deemed the worst environmental disaster in Europe since Chernobyl. Wildlife probably won't return to normal until 2010.

TOURS AND EXCURSIONS IN THE DANUBE AREA

For equipment hire and organized caving trips around Belogradchik, contact the **Caving Club Bel Prilep**, tel: (0936) 32-85.
Magura Cave, tel: (0936) 31-61, www.magura.hit.bg
For boat cruises, bus tours around the region and car rentals, contact **Danube Tours Rousse**, 5 Khan Kubrat St, tel: (082) 82-5048, www.dunavtours.bg
For Silistra river cruises, bookings can be made at the **Hotel Zlatna Dobrudja**.

DUROSTORUM

It's hard to believe that the ruins you see in the pedestrianized park between the town centre and the Danube are from the prosperous Roman-Byzantine fortified city Durostorum (early 2nd century AD). After centuries of efflorescence it finally succumbed to the eastern Barbarian tribes – the Slavs and the Bulgars – in the 7th century. Khan Asparuh, the founder of the Bulgarian state, rebuilt it as Drustur. It was here that in the 10th century Bulgaria, Byzantium and Kiev Russia fought the battle that ended in Byzantine victory and occupation for almost two centuries. The double-headed eagle on coins and jewellery in the museum was the symbol of Bulgarian Despot Ivanko Terter in the decades before Bulgaria fell to the Ottomans.

Roman Tomb ★★★

This is the only preserved major Roman tomb in Bulgaria. The 4th-century murals depict the master couple and their servants, hunting scenes and the dead patrician himself. Open on request, for groups only, tel: (086) 82-0386.

Medjidi Tabia Fortress ★★★

Built on top of a Roman fortress with forced Bulgarian labour, this fascinating Turkish fort was the work of a Prussian military engineer in the mid-19th century and played a key role in the Crimean War (1953–56) and later in the Russian-Turkish war (1877–78) which liberated Bulgaria. It housed successive garrisons for 100 years and the graffiti of no less than eight nationalities are scribbled on the stone walls. It was named after Sultan Abdul Medjid after his visit in 1847. In the early years of Communist dictatorship, 'enemies of the people' were imprisoned and tortured here. Open 08:00–20:00, tel: (086) 82-0269. It is located 5km (3 miles) south of town; get a taxi. You can hike in the green hillside.

Archaeological Museum ★★

This interesting and well-presented museum was originally built as a bank in the 1920s when the northeast was Romanian territory. There are no English explanations but even so, it's not hard to spot the curious Thracian necropolis with skeletons buried in foetal positions, the gladiator helmets and fragments from a chariot, the gold Roman jewellery, the altar to Emperor Marcus Aurelius, and the mountains of coins from Despot Terter's rule. Open 09:00–12:00, 13:00–17:30 Tue–Sat, winter Tue–Fri.

Sveshtari Tomb★★

On the inland Road 23 between Ruse and Silistra is one of Bulgaria's best-known Thracian tombs, a World Heritage site. As with the Kazanlâk Tomb, the focus of interest is the 3rd-century BC relief mural in the burial chamber, here depicting 10 caryatids (maidens), and the beautiful painted murals above. Some archaeologists believe that this was the burial site of King Drumihed, of the Thracian tribe Getes. Visits by previous arrangement only.

The Danube at a Glance

Late spring/ early summer (May–Jun) and early autumn (Sep) are best, and high summer if you don't mind heat.

From Sofia to Belogradchik/ Vidin, the E79 is best, but the road following the Iskâr Gorge is gorgeous. Get to Ruse via E85 from Veliko Târnovo and E70 from Varna. A good road runs between Ruse and Silistra.

Private transport is best. Regular buses go between Belogradchik and Vidin, and between Ruse and Silistra, but they are often shabby. The smaller sights are accessible only by private car. Secondary roads aren't great.

Belogradchik
BUDGET
Madonna Inn and Restaurant, up the hill along Hristo Botev St from main square, tel: (0936) 55-46, www.madonainn-bg. com Friendly family hotel with glorious view and home-cooked food. Tours and cycling organized with advance notice.
Turisticheski Dom, 10 minutes' walk down the road from main square, past the Rocks, tel: (0936) 33-82. Dated but adequate, in picturesque setting. Sauna, restaurant, café, gym.

Vidin
LUXURY
Hotel Anna-Kristina, 2 Baba Vida St, tel: (094) 60-6038,

www.annakristinahotel.com Renovated 19th-century bath-house in the Park, good value. Steam-room, summer pool, restaurant, summer garden.
MID-RANGE
The Old Town Hotel, 2 Knyaz Boris St, tel: (094) 60-0023, www.oldtownhotel.dir.bg Impeccable family hotel near Stambul Capia gates.
Bononia, 2 Bdin St (near main square), tel: (094) 60-6031, moira_bg200@yahoo.com Comfortable and convenient. Bar, restaurant, café, parking.

Ruse
LUXURY
Danube Plaza Hotel, 5 Svoboda Sq, tel: (082) 29-29, www.danubeplaza.com 80 comfortable rooms in great location, good European restaurant, sauna, gym.
Anna Palace, 4 Knyajeska St, (opposite Sexaginta Prista), tel: (082) 82-5005, www.anna palace.com Retro boutique hotel in restored period mansion. Has a fascinating history.
MID-RANGE
Riga Hotel, 22 Pridunavski St on the waterfront, tel: (082) 22-181. Large renovated hotel, all rooms with Danube views.
Charlino, Dunav Sq, tel: (082) 82-5706, charlino@ruse. techno-link.com Pleasant boutique hotel in quiet plaza just west of main square.
BUDGET
Kapriz, Khan Kubrat Sq. Five comfortable rooms in a quiet courtyard (except for the disco next door).

Silistra
LUXURY
Hotel Drustar, 10 Cap. Mamarchev St along waterfront, tel: (086) 81-2200, www.hotel drustar.com Swanky beauty salon, pool, bars, restaurant.
BUDGET
Hotel Zlatna Dobrudja, 1 Dobrudja St, tel: (086) 82-1357. Partly renovated, uninspiring hotel in the centre.

Belogradchik
Madonna Inn (see Where to Stay). **Restaurant Elite**, 200m up the road from Madonna Inn, tel: (0936) 45-58. Bulgarian cuisine in pleasant ambience.
Vidin
Evergreen, 4 Vitosha St, tel: (094) 60-0342. Pleasant garden, good traditional dishes.
Riviera, only restaurant in the park, tel: 0888-400209. Large Bulgarian menu, Danube views.
Ruse
Lovna Sreshta, Hotel Kapriz, European food, game dishes.
Leventa, tel: (082) 86-2880. Winery, traditional food, music.
Silistra
Cafés and restaurants along the pedestrian mall, Hotel Zlatna Dobrudja, and Hotel Drustar.

Belogradchik Tourist Centre, town square, tel: (0936) 42-94.
Ruse Tourist Info Centre for Rusenski Lom info, (082) 82-5002, 60 Aleksandrovska St, closed weekends.
Rusenski Lom information centre, tel: (082) 27-2397.

Travel Tips

Tourist Information

For package bookings from the UK, contact Balkan Holidays in London, tel: +44 20 754-35569, www.balkanholidays.co.uk The Bulgarian Tourist Authority, Sv Nedelya Sq 1, Sofia, tel: +359 2 987 9778, www.bulgariatravel.org has no representatives outside the country.

www.visittobulgaria.com has information on practicalities as well as destinations, and a list of travel agencies in Bulgaria. The best thing to do is contact individual tour operators in Bulgaria to tailor your holiday. Local travel agencies are listed in the 'At a Glance' sections. These **specialist tour operators** are all based in Sofia, except Branta Tours. All of them can be (and some of them should be) contacted before you arrive.

Mountain, rural, eco-tourism, monasteries: Odysseia-In, bul. Stamboliiski 20B, tel: (02) 98-90538, www.odysseia-in.com. Tailor-made itineraries for groups and individuals. Zig-Zag Holidays, bul. Stamboliiski 20B, (02) 98-05102, www.zigzagbg.com

Bird-watching and wildlife tours along the seacoast: Branta Tours, tel: (05743) 2259, www.branta-tours.com

Wildlife, botanical, cycling and hiking tours: Spatia Tours, Slaveikov Sq 2, floor 2, tel: (02) 98-61212, http://wildlife.spatia-tour.com

Outdoor activities, cultural itineraries: Alexander Tour, 44 Pop Bogomil St, tel: (02) 98-33322, www.alexandertour.com

Monastery, icon, wine-tasting and other cultural tours: Yomex, 12A Ivan Vazov St, tel: (02) 98-10956, www.yomexbg.com Caters for business travellers and groups.

Entry Requirements

EU nationals normally don't need a visa for stays of up to 90 days. Nationals of Australia, Canada, Israel, Japan, New Zealand, UK and USA don't need visas for up to 30 days. Other nationals must check with their nearest Bulgarian Embassy before travel.

Customs

Duty-free allowances are the same as in other EU countries: 1 litre of spirits, 2 litres of wine, 200 cigarettes. Currency above 8000 lv must be declared. You are not allowed to export antiques, numismatic coins or artworks without a permit from the Ministry of Culture. Small children accompanying you must demonstrably be yours (on paper), due to precautions against child-trafficking. Pets must have valid certificates of recent vet examination. If arriving in a private car, you must have an ownership certificate and all other relevant papers. Sofia and Varna International Airports have good duty-free shopping areas at quite competitive prices.

Getting There

By Air: There are three international airports: in Sofia, Varna and Burgas. Most major and some minor European airlines fly to Sofia. British Airways and Bulgaria Air are the best choices from the UK. Bulgaria Air flies from most European capitals. Charter airlines like Bulgaria Air Charter service the Black Sea in summer, and some European airlines fly to Varna and Burgas International Airports. Hemus Air flies from Beirut, Dubai and Tripoli.

By road: The E79 road from Greece through Kulata checkpoint is in excellent condition. The picturesque E87 from Turkey to the Black Sea coast passes through Strandja Mountain. The E80 from Turkey to Sofia is also scenic and runs through Plovdiv. International buses from Europe are a comfortable option; they all pass through

Serbia and Montenegro and checkpoint procedure can be painfully slow.

By rail: The cheapest and slowest way of travelling from Western Europe. The train from Istanbul or Athens/Thessaloniki is a comfortable option.

By boat: Crossing the Danube from Romania, you'll arrive in Ruse or Vidin. Ruse is a nice introduction to the country.

What to Pack

Good ear plugs to ward off noise pollution, especially along the Black Sea coast in summer; a plug adaptor if necessary (see Electricity); a sink plug if you use such things (Bulgarians consider it unhygienic so you won't find plugs anywhere). Bring good hiking shoes if you intend to venture out in the mountains. If you're on a special diet, bring foods and supplements, as speciality health shops are thin on the ground (there are a few in Sofia). Most other things you forget, you can buy in Sofia.

Money Matters

The currency is the lev, which is divided into 100 stotinki. It has been stable for the last few years. Always have smaller notes on you – don't pay taxi drivers and food stalls in 50 lev notes because they don't have enough change. In Sofia's Vitosha St, every second shop is a change bureau; all of them are fine, but the street changers aren't – just avoid them. The major currencies are the US dollar and the euro. Go to a bank to exchange other currencies. Most luxury hotels also exchange money. Travellers' cheques are easily changed, and there are cash-points in every town which accept international Visa and Master cards. Credit cards are accepted in luxury hotels and restaurants, luxury shops, and rent-a-car agencies. Make sure you always have cash on you.

Accommodation

The standard of accommodation is high throughout the country, and almost always good or excellent value for money. This is not to say that choices are always plentiful. In towns like Belogradchik luxury hasn't arrived yet, and in Burgas budget lodgings are non-existent. Shared bathrooms are a very rare occurrence, even in rock-bottom hotels. Some tourist hot-spots – Plovdiv, Veliko Târnovo, Bansko, the sea resorts - are dramatically more expensive than the rest of the country, especially during the season. Star-rating does little except to indicate there is a satellite TV in your room, so always inspect the room first. The best mid-range and budget options are boutique and family hotels (the Bulgarian version of B&B, which doesn't always offer the second B). These usually have all the comforts plus a homely atmosphere and friendly hosts – this is often nicer, not to mention cheaper, than an impersonal refurbished Balkantourist hotel or a faceless brand-new affair in a hotel ghetto. Hotels rarely have tea and coffee making facilities in the room, except for some family hotels.

In some family hotels, it is possible to hire a car from your hosts for the day or ask them to take you sightseeing.

Eating Out

Bigger towns like Veliko Târnovo and tourist spots like Bansko and Sozopol have a good range of eateries, and cities like Sofia, Varna and Plovdiv will spoil you for choice. It is now easy to find world cuisine in Sofia, from Mexican to Japanese, but the

ROAD SIGNS

Road signs on motorways and first class roads usually appear in both Cyrillic and Latin script. On secondary roads they usually don't, so it's a good idea to learn the Cyrillic alphabet and get a reliable road map. Travel map of Bulgaria by Domino (red cover) is recommended. On tertiary roads, signs are sporadic to say the least.

rest of the country is still much very attached to its traditional fare of Bulgarian/Balkan dishes and the ubiquitous pizza, pasta and kebabs. In the summer and autumn, the food stalls come out – corn on the cob, roasted nuts and chestnuts, crêpes. The serving order in all but the most chic restaurants is sporadic: usually, everything comes out at once, so make a point of requesting your courses separately. Tipping at your discretion is recommended, all the more that prices are ridiculously low by Western standards, as are wages. Restaurants are busy by 8pm.

Transport

By air: Travelling in Bulgaria by air is only recommended if you are very pressed for time, as going by road is infinitely more interesting. There are several daily flights from Sofia to Varna and Burgas in the summer, and daily flights the rest of the year.

By road: Seeing the country by car is the interesting way go, but once you get off the main highways and first class roads, it can be fraught with shocking roads, missing or incomprehensible road signs, and reckless drivers. You need an international driving license or a certified translation of your license. You also need a vignette, a road tax disc, to drive on the open roads. This is obtained at border checkpoints, petrol stations and post offices. Petrol or *benzin* is slightly cheaper than in other EU countries. Speed limits are 120 kph (75 mph) on motorways, 90 kph (56 mph) on other roads, and 50 kph (31 mph) in populated areas. Some roads, however, are so bad that you wouldn't – or shouldn't – reach the speed limit. If you are stopped by

road police in a private car, you must show registration and ownership papers, your passport, and international motor insurance (which can be taken out at the border). If you are fined, you don't have to pay cash on the spot – ask for a written fine, and pay it later at customs. Rental cars from various companies including Hertz, Budget, Avis, and the Bulgarian Tany 97 are readily available in every city and luxury hotel, and at Sofia Airport.

By bus: The bus network is extensive, the travel cost is extremely low, and buses connecting bigger/tourist towns are of a good standard. In less touristy areas or smaller towns, however, they can resemble war wrecks. Some villages and natural sights like caves are not accessible by bus and are best reached by taxi (*see below*). The only problem you'll encounter is deciphering chalk-scribbled timetables at provincial bus stations. This, however, is not a problem at the excellent Sofia Central Bus Station where you can get printed timetables for major destinations. Buses leave on time, so don't be late. **Sofia Central Bus Station**, tel: 0900 21000 (24 hours), check www.central naavtogara.bg for timetables.

Taxis: Cheap and plentiful, taxis are the best alternative to a private car. They are a good way to make day trips and to move between towns instead of grappling with bus timetables. Negotiate a rate with the driver before you set off on bigger trips. In Sofia and most other towns, taxis are metered.

CONVERSION CHART

From	To	Multiply By
Millimetres	Inches	0.0394
Metres	Yards	1.0936
Metres	Feet	3.281
Kilometres	Miles	0.6214
Square kilometres	Square miles	0.386
Hectares	Acres	2.471
Litres	Pints	1.760
Kilograms	Pounds	2.205
Tonnes	Tons	0.984

To convert Celsius to Fahrenheit: x 9 ÷ 5 + 32

By train: This is the slowest way to move across the country, and the cheapest. It is often very scenic and almost always social as you get to meet the people in your compartment. Most towns and villages are linked by railways, but again – you'll run into timetables in Bulgarian only, disruptions, repair works, and sleepy provincial clerks. Trains are increasingly supplanted by the more convenient buses, and now only old people and those on low incomes will take the train (which still makes for a lot of people). If you do take a train, buy a first class ticket to ensure you get a seat. You can buy a ticket on the spot at the railway station, as trains are never full, or in central Sofia at **Rila Bureau**, 5 Gurko St (next to the Central Post Office). Keep an eye on your luggage at all times and be prepared for shocking train toilets. Restaurant wagons are unpredictable, so bring your own food and drink.

Business Hours
Banks and financial institutions 09:00–16:00. Shops 09:00 or 10:00–19:00 or 20:00, some open on Saturday too, rarely on Sunday. Offices 09:00–17:00. Museums and sights vary, and often close for lunch.

Time Difference
GMT + 2; summertime GMT + 3.

Communications
To avoid the surcharges of hotel phones, use street phones with cards purchased at any kiosk. Internet is widely available – Internet cafés and joints can be found in most towns and villages, and sometimes you can also make phone calls there. There are three mobile GSM networks – Mobitel, Globul, and Vivatel – and pre-paid cards can be bought at kiosks or mobile phone shops. Posting anything bigger than a postcard is a chore. Stamps, including for postcards, must be bought at post offices. The Sofia Central Post Office, Dyakon Ignatii St (near Slaveikov Square), is open during business hours, but sending a parcel involves 3 different queues and surprising amounts of money. Use Fedex, tel: 94-29400, or Aramex International Courier, tel: 98-71111.

Electricity
220V, 50 Hz. European style, two round pin plugs are used.

Weights and Measures
The metric system is used.

Health Precautions
There are no health risks involved in visiting Bulgaria except possible tummy upset from dodgy tap water along the Black Sea. Bulgaria's tap water is potable, but stick to mineral water along the seaside and, if necessary, elsewhere too. Have ample sun protection in the summer and during winter sports, especially high in the mountains where the sun is a killer. Food is generally safe, even at street stalls, and if you do get funny guts, it'll likely be just the change of diet.

Health Services
Avoid public health services which are overstretched and under-funded; private clinics are of a European standard. You'll need travel insurance. Dentists are good value and work to a high standard, but it's best to have a recommendation from someone local.

Personal Safety
Bulgaria is safe for travellers. But watch out for bad drivers and street muggers. Markets are popular with pickpockets, so

THE CYRILLIC ALPHABET

Аа	Aa	ask
Бб	Bb	Bulgaria
Вв	Vv	very
Гг	Gg	great
Дд	Dd	drink
Ее	Ee	ever
Жж	Jj	treasure
Зз	Zz	Zulu
Ии	Ii	inn
Йй	Yy	you
Лл	Ll	lemon
Мм	Mm	mine
Нн	Nn	not
Оо	Oo	rot
Пп	Pp	Plovdiv
Рр	Rr	rat
Сс	Ss	Sofia
Тт	Tt	ten
Уу	Uu	boo
Фф	Ff	fair
Хх	Hh	loch
Цц	'ts'	lots
Чч	'ch'	chop
Шш	'sh'	shop
Щщ	'sht'	mashed
Ъъ	'u'	burn
Ьь	not pronounced, used to soften the 'o'	
Юю	'yu'	you
Яя	'ya'	yang

USEFUL PHRASES

Hello – *dobâr den*
Goodbye – *dovijdane* or *ciao* (informal)
How are you? – *kak ste?* or *kak si?* (informal)
I'm well – *dobre sâm*
OK – *dobre*
Thank you – *blagodarya* or *merci*
Yes – *da* (shake your head)
No – *ne* (nod)
I want – *iskam*
I don't want – *ne iskam*
Please/ you're welcome/ I beg your pardon? – *molya*
Very nice/good – *mnogo hubavo*
Cheers! – *nazdrave!*

always keep an eye on your possessions. If you see stray dogs – a common sight in Bulgarian streets – avoid them to be on the safe side. Otherwise, use your common sense and sensitivity and don't display expensive watches and jewellery, or carry excessive amounts of cash on you. Avoid going to deserted areas at night.

Emergencies

Emergency 150 or 515-31; Police 166; Road assistance 91146; Fire brigade 160. Employees might speak English but don't count on it.

Etiquette

Being polite, friendly and open will be to your advantage – Bulgarians are friendly to foreigners, but sometimes too shy to initiate contact. Bulgaria is a relaxed modern country and most things go in Sofia. In small towns and villages, greet older

people in the street with *dobâr den*. When introduced to strangers, you may shake hands with both men and women. Friends sometimes kiss (though not two men). Bulgarian women always dress up when going out, but as a tourist you'll be forgiven for wearing practical garb. When entering churches, women are expected to cover their shoulders. When invited into people's homes, it is customary to remove your shoes unless instructed otherwise. Never turn up at somebody's house empty-handed – flowers, chocolates, wine or fruit are common gifts.

Language

Bulgarian is the national language, and Turkish is spoken in some areas by the Turkish ethnic minority. English is spoken to some degree by most

PUBLIC HOLIDAYS

1 January – New Year's Day
3 March – Liberation Day
8–9 April – Eastern Orthodox Easter (date varies)
1 May – Labour Day
6 May – Bulgarian Army Day
24 May – Day of St Cyril and St Methodius (Day of Slavonic culture and literacy)
6 September – Reunification Day (1885)
22 September – Independence Day (1878)
24 December – Christmas Eve
25–26 December – Christmas Day and Boxing Day

younger Bulgarians, and German or French by some older people. Russian is universally understood, but a few words of Bulgarian will bring out smiles that Russian definitely won't.

GOOD READING

Conrad, Joseph (1899) *Lord Jim*, Penguin.
Barnes, Julian (1993) *The Porcupine*, Picador. Allegorical account of the trial of a totalitarian dictator, set in Bulgaria.
Buxton, Christopher (2006) *Far from the Danube*, Kronos, Sofia. A historical drama about the real-life romance between a Bulgarian noblewoman and a French Crusader in 14th-century Europe.
Gospodinov, Georgi (2005) *Natural Novel*, Dalkey Archive Press. Experimental novel by a Bulgarian author narrated by a hapless protagonist.
Groueff, Stephane (1998) *Crown of Thorns*, Madison Books. A history of the reign of the tragic Tsar Boris III of Bulgaria (1918–43).
Hoffman, Eva (1994) *Exit into History*, Penguin. Travel essays on the changed face of post-Communist Eastern Europe, including Bulgaria.
Kostova, Elizabeth (2005) *The Historian*, Little Brown. Literary thriller about the 'real' Dracula, partly set in 1960s Bulgaria.
Shkodrova, Albena & **Georgieff, Anthony** (2006) *Hidden Treasures of Bulgaria*, Mediacorp Ltd, Sofia. A lively, smart, practical alternative guide to off-the-beaten-track Bulgaria, with photographs. Bilingual.
White, Jonathan (2005) *Buying a Property in Bulgaria*, How to Books. Practical advice from first-hand experience, written with humour.

INDEX